Book Two

Milo, Me and The Beast

The Middle...

By Nicci Taylor

I dedicate this book to Harper, my Granddaughter. May she too have a life full of opportunities and adventures.

As always, I must first thank Milo, without whom, my adventures could never happen. And my Beast, who provided Milo and Me with our safe haven throughout our travels. I am forever grateful to my wonderful family and close friends who are always there, holding a safety net, just in case. Pip, my sister and forever friend throughout. My mum, who still asks "when will this mid-life crisis end?" And my son, Philip, who probably still denies knowing me! Thank you to Jefferson Merrick, my editor, for making my books readable. And an ongoing thank you to my friends, old and new, through social media, who continue to follow my adventure. And last of all I thank Me. Me, who had a dream. Me, who believed in my dream. And Me, who is still, forever dreaming. Never give up on your dream...

Chapter 1

The Beast rocked slightly from side to side while the rain tip-tapped on the roof. I looked over at Milo, snoring contently on the left hand couch, twitching occasionally whilst doggy dreaming. He looked so cute, wrapped up in one of my mum's oversized t-shirt's, oblivious to the bright pink fabric. I probably didn't look much better, wearing my fleecy lined Primark leggings, long thermal socks up to my knees, a big thick knobbly cardigan and all topped off with my bargain bought, size 20 dressing-gown. But it was so cold outside and although I'd tried my best to block every draught sneaking into our motor-home a chill hung menacingly in the air.

Having run out of cushions, by using them all to block the drafts, I'd now resorted to rolling up my bath towels to stuff along the edge of the windows. Milo opened one eye and watched me from the couch.

"Sorry, Baby, did I wake you?" I asked.

Milo yawned, made a cute squeaky noise and repositioned himself into a ball, tucking his nose under his tail. He was fine.

I caught a glimpse of myself as I passed the mirror and marvelled at how tanned my face still was. My all-over sun-kissed glow had remained, even though I'd left San Pedro three weeks ago. But now the majority of it lay hidden, beneath layer upon layer of clothing.

"I've got white bits Milo, but I doubt anyone will ever see them" I moaned. He didn't flicker.

I sat down beside him and cuddled in for some body-heat. Having left the sunny hot climate of South America, the cold British winter had arrived, and here I was; living in my motor-home, the Beast, with Milo, in my mum's back garden.

I reflected on how things can change at the 'drop of a hat'. During the last year my life had been like a mini roller-coaster. Having made a bold decision, less than a year ago, to give up my home, sell everything I owned, buy a motor-home and go looking for a husband, I now found myself with no address, no furniture, and sadly no husband. How funny.

I certainly had no regrets about my past, I'd had an absolute ball with Milo and our Beast, and had created some amazing memories during our adventure. I'd seen landscapes I didn't know existed, met people from all walks of life and experienced a lifestyle outside of my comfort zone. OK, so I didn't find myself a husband but I'd had a jolly good time trying. And I wasn't ready to give up. Living in my mum's back garden, in a motor-home, with a dog was not the end of the world. It was temporary. The 'hat' would drop again.

"I've got a plan Milo." Milo lifted his head and his ears pricked up.

"We're going on another adventure, me and you, we're going to Ireland in the Beast." I told him. "Would you like that, Milo?".

Milos head tilted from side to side, as I spoke, and I marvelled at how handsome he looked when he did this. Over the years I'd learnt to recognise which words Milo responded to the most. The popular word being 'would'. If I ever included the word 'would' into a sentence, then Milos attention was guaranteed. This mainly being down to the fact that his food had always been offered as; "Would you like your dinner?" "Would you like a biscuit?" or "Would you like a piece of my toast?". I don't think he ever heard past the word would, because as soon as it was spoken, he'd be sitting at my feet in anticipation.

Milo sat patiently at my feet, his tail wagging and his eyes wanting. Yes, I thought to myself, Milo would love an adventure in Ireland; but not before a biscuit.

I'd loved Milo from day one but since we'd been living together in our motor-home, I'd grown to love him even more. Living in such a small space could have caused untold mayhem, but with Milo it was fine. We both fitted in perfectly together. Travelling to Ireland would be a perfect adventure.

So, I had a destination but the plan was a bit blurry. I originally wanted to travel to Italy. A place I'd visited often, and which held a special place in my heart. But as my motor-home bore all the signs of old age and had no air-conditioning, I decided Italy would be the wrong choice. Ireland it was then, we would take the ferry from Liverpool to Dublin and then drive down the coast and keep on driving until I found myself a husband.

I loved all the various Irish accents, their sense of humour and that Irish look of dark hair and piercing blue eyes. Surely, I would find the man of my dreams there? Holed up in mum's garden on the Wirral, as if in hibernation, was not where I should be. Having previously lived on the Wirral for over ten years with a track record resulting in little luck on the love front meant my journey just had to continue. The adventure of Milo and Me was not over yet. Or as my mum would say "When is this mid-life crisis going to end?"

She thinks I look cute! I'm wearing a bright pink t-shirt and she's taking photographs. I'm a five-year-old, Fox Red Labrador for goodness sake, it clashes with my fur, and it belongs to her mother. I look ridiculous and just pray none of the other dogs find out about this. Mind you, it does smell rather nice. I'm picking up the faint trace of a Tunnock Tea Cake, her mother does rather like them.

To be honest I don't really mind how I look. I'm just glad Mee is back. I'm not sure where she went but she was gone rather a long time. Mee always tells me "I'm just going to the shops, Baby." then she kisses me, hugs me, hugs me again, pops me a biscuit, usually followed by another kiss and then off she goes. Sometimes she isn't gone long but sometimes it can be ages. This time it was ages. She left me with her mother, where I became aware of the Tunnock Tea Cakes and also how wobbly she is on her feet.

Now Mee tells me she has a plan. She looked so happy telling me this. Her face lit up and she looked so pretty, for a human that is. Apparently, we are going on another adventure, in our Beast. We are going to a place called Ireland.

Someone asked me recently why I call her 'Mee'. Duh! Because that is her name. I learnt this from an early age, with her constant commands of; "give it to Mee" "wait for Mee" "follow Mee" "look at Mee". Even her blog is called Milo and Mee.

Chapter 2

Mum's back garden was not the biggest of spaces. In fact, it was just a yard. An area of paved space between her house and her garage to be precise. Squeezing the Beast in was not easy and entailed removing her gate and one fence panel. But Mum kindly let me do this and even kinder of her: she let me plug into her electric supply. I loved my mum to bits but as a grown up approaching fifty it just seemed wrong to be living in her house. Plus, she was dodgy on her hips and Milo kept knocking her over.

So, after a fair bit of manoeuvring we eventually got the Beast in the yard. I felt quite content and cosy, slotted in between the two buildings, although my mums view from her living room window was now just the side of my van. But she never complained.

"Will you be okay there, love?" Mum asked.

"Yes, Mum, its perfect." I replied.

"Is your handbrake on? I don't want you rolling into next door's garden."

"Yes, Mum, my handbrake is on." I assured her.

Mum worried about me on a regular basis. She would tap on my door most days with items of food, extra blankets, treats for Milo or just to check I was still alive. One day she brought me a large sheet of blue tarpaulin. She insisted I wrap it around the Beast to keep out the drafts. And my word what a difference it made. It did look a bit daft, stuck down with gaffer tape, but I didn't care. No more drafts.

Milo settled into our new life quite well. As long as he got his early morning walk, he was happy to just chill in the van. His favourite spot being the conservatory i.e. the front passenger seat, head on the dashboard, the winter sun beating through the glass. We both loved our conservatory area, the dashboard displayed a vase of fake yellow roses, a few ornaments and drip mats for my coffee cups. I would chill in the driver's seat for hours, reading my books or listening to the radio, Milo always by my side curled up on the passenger seat. From here, Milo had a perfect view into my mum's house and could see whenever she ventured into her kitchen. I always knew if my mum was in her kitchen because Milo would run to my door, whining to be let out. He would then sit at my mum's back door and watch her through the glass, cooking. He would sit there, rain or shine, boring his big, sad, Labrador eyes into hers, until she succumbed and threw him some scraps.

I had now secured myself a job at The Manor, a local, fine dining restaurant I'd visited often with my family. A pleasant well-run establishment, with a great bunch of staff and they'd offered me the position of barmaid. With a regular weekly pay packet, I could now build up my fund to travel to Ireland. Plus, my shifts didn't start too early thus enabling me to walk Milo in the mornings before I left.

Living in my mum's back garden, my overheads were relatively low. Apart from the massive credit card debt I'd built up whilst travelling. The bane of my life. That bugger was going to follow me for years. But, I figured, from my wages at the restaurant I should hopefully have enough money to start travelling by early Spring.

I was not the best barmaid. In fact, rubbish would be a better description. I lost count of how many drinks I spilled over the customers. Whenever we received a drink order we had to carry it over to the customers table on a round tray. We had to position all the drinks on the tray to achieve some kind of balance and then carry it on the palm of one hand to the table. On arriving at the table, having usually lost the top layer of the lager pints en route, we would place each drink next to the appropriate customer. The worst thing would be if they tried to help by removing their drink from the tray, thus unbalancing my tray.

On one particular evening having reached a table of customers I leant over to place their drinks down. Unfortunately, as I did so, a gentleman knocked me with his elbow and I watched, in slow motion, as his pint of beer first wobbled and then threw itself through the air tipping its entire contents into his lap. I automatically grabbed the nearest napkin and proceeded to wipe him down, at which point his wife got quite hysterical and snatched the napkin from me. I apologised profusely and my manager offered them all free drinks as compensation. They chose to kick up quite a stink at the end of the evening and left without paying any of their bill.

Situations like this happened to me on a regular basis and I never got the hang of those trays; but I believed my customer service skills were excellent. That is until I read a Trip Advisor complaint about me: I'd only been in the job for about a week when a lady approached me asking if there was wheelchair access for her husband, into the building? I informed her there was but as I was unsure of which entrance offered the best access, I would check with my manager. He then explained to her that although the restaurant was, at this point, empty, we were in fact fully booked. But he was more than happy to offer her a lower level bar table for her and her husband. She then left and didn't return.

About three days later, the manager showed me the on-line complaint. She basically said I was rude and useless, had turned away custom and, worst of all, she wrote "She had obviously never seen a 'brown' person before." I'm never rude, I'd clarified wheelchair access with my manager, she was offered a table and I am the least racist person I know.

I felt so upset by this complaint, but my manager pointed out that her Trip Advisor record showed she had made regular complaints at various restaurants, so don't take it personally. But I did.

Some days I was taken off the bar and asked to work on the floor serving food to the tables. No doubt a cost cutting exercise in my managers mind. I always admired how the other waitresses could carry three or four plates up the length of their arms. I could never manage more than one plate in each hand, but compensated this by running a lot faster than them.

Initially, I did think working on the bar I might come across the man of my dreams. That he might just float in one evening, order an expensive bottle of champagne, ask me to share it with him and then declare his undying love for me. It never happened. Most of the customers were either families, couples or groups of females. One particular evening a young man stood at the bar and said to me, "It's Nicci isn't it? You remember me?"

I studied him for a moment, wondering who on earth he was. Then I remembered.

"Oh, Hi." I replied "Yes, I remember you. I remember picking you up drunk from many a pub"

His parents, who were standing next to him, just stared at me with a look of horror on their faces.

"Oh, God! No! Not like that. I mean when he used to go drinking with my son. Years ago." I tried to explain. "I was a Mum taxi." They continued to stare at me whilst the young man grinned and said, "Say Hi to Phil for me." His parents glared over at me for the remainder of the evening.

This is going to be a speedy result. It's raining and mother always responds quicker if it's raining. I'm giving her my best, sad Labrador eyes, with an added little whimper for effect. She knows I'm there, any minute now she will turn around, spot my forlorn little face in her window and wobble over with a bit of whatever it is she's cooking. I think it's toast. Oh, I do hope so, I love toast. And here she comes! There is definitely something in her hand, I do wish she could wobble a bit quicker, I'm starving. Must remember not to snatch, that's the hard bit, I can never get it in my mouth quick enough. And chew, they always seem upset when I swallow it whole, I don't know why it upsets them, because it all lands in my tummy eventually. Yes! It was toast, I even managed to give it a quick chew before swallowing, which resulted in a 'good-boy' from the mother. Happy days, now back to the van to chill out in the conservatory.

Chapter 3

Spring approached and our imminent departure for Ireland loomed closer . I'd done a bit of research on-line and written a list of must-visit places. One of these being 'the magic road' in County Waterford. Apparently, you can 'roll' uphill in your vehicle. The thought of this intrigued me and I imagined it would be worth seeing the Beast roll uphill. I'd also listed a visit to Father Ted's house in County Clare and a trip to Dingle Harbour, hoping to see the famous dolphin named Fungie. I also planned to cover most of the Wild Atlantic Way on our journey, which would hopefully provide us with some stunning coastal locations.

During this on-line research I'd come upon a website called Safe Nights Ireland (SNI). This website offered a list of places providing a safe location to stay in your motor-home, for a nominal fee of ten euros. The list included pubs, farms or even a person's home. You were guaranteed a safe place to park and use of a water supply and sometimes electricity. I thought this was a good idea and signed up to join.

Having written of my planned adventure in my blog I now had an impressive amount of people inviting me to visit them during my tour of Ireland. My invitations ranged from friendly families, lovely couples and interested gentlemen. I replied to each and every one, thanking them for their kind invitations. I had also, yet again, attracted some media attention. Some days were now spent doing radio interviews with various local stations in Ireland and arranging TV appearances and newspaper interviews to take place during my travels. This was all fine by me, hoping in the back of my mind, that this could potentially lead to meeting the man of my dreams; He could be listening and like the sound of my voice, he could read about me and like what he read or he could see my picture and like what he saw. Anything that would help to bring me closer to my happy ever after.

Researching on-line I read that Milo needed his own passport for travel to Ireland. Luckily, I found out in time, as this had to be processed at least twenty-one days before travel. So, having sat in the vets for over an hour, for just a five-minute appointment, I was now nearly one hundred pounds lighter. But Milo was now in possession of his very own passport with his cutest photo displayed on the inside pages. Also, whilst on-line, I found the ferry prices were not coming in cheap, so I went ahead and booked our ticket to Dublin, before they increased any more. With a confirmed booking and the thought of driving the Beast onto a large ship terrifying me slightly, I added a note onto my booking stating 'nervous female driver, travelling with an equally nervous dog', hoping this would afford me some 'special attention'.

Having ruled out Italy as a travel destination, thinking it would be far too difficult, I was now trying to sort out passports, rabies jabs, foreign currency, sim cards for my phone, using my bank card outside the UK and various other incidentals for travelling abroad. Not quite hop on a ferry and go. I'd also discovered the caravan club membership I'd paid for had only two camp-sites in Ireland. Added to this, having watched some on-line videos with Discover Ireland, I was struggling to understand the various Irish accents. Stress mode began to kick in.

Stressed and scared of what lay ahead, my doubts began to set in. Less than a year ago I'd sold everything I owned, given up my job, bought a motor-home and driven off to Scotland with Milo. All my anticipations were unknown. I had little fear or doubt as I did not know what lay ahead of me. My ignorance had been bliss. Now I was scared. I had insight as to what *could* happen. My mind was going into overdrive: What if the ferry sinks? What if Milo gets lost? What if a wheel falls off the Beast? What if I run out of money? What if no-one likes me?

I poured out my woes to my sister, Pip.

"The ferry has lifeboats. Milo never leaves your side. You have RAC cover. You have a credit card. And who on earth could not like you, Nicci?" Pip said trying to reassure me.

"I know, I know. I just seem to have so many 'what if's' this time. I thought it would be easier having experienced it already. But having that insight has brought the opposite effect." I told her.

"Nicci, you're my crazy little sister and I love you to bits. You're living the dream, your dream. There is nothing holding you back unless you let it." Pip reinforced.

I knew this. I knew I was extremely fortunate to be able to follow my dream. I was well aware of how many people could not do what I was doing: They wrote to me on a daily basis. I was also aware of how some people thought I was crazy. Crazy for wanting to live in a tin box on wheels, never knowing where you would sleep at night and in constant search of a happy ever after. But I believed I had opportunity lying at my feet and I could bend down and pick it up or I could step over it. It was my choice, I had the choice. This was my mid-life crisis and I was determined to make the most of it.

To prove to myself I wasn't a complete disaster on the dating scene I decided to give online dating another try. With a glass of wine poured and Milo by my side I sat in my van scrutinizing the online profiles of suitable men. As usual my scrutinizing went far too deep; little things such as multiple spelling mistakes, ignorant held beliefs or even the fact that I'd be looking down at them if I wore high-heels, were just some of the reasons to put me off most of the available men. The more I looked the more my list of unacceptable traits grew. After a few hours of scrolling I wondered if I should just close my eyes and hit enter on my keypad? The likely hood was I would never find anyone who could match my tick list because; people do not always represent themselves well on paper. But just because a gentleman has spelt 'there, they're or their' incorrectly does not mean we couldn't live happily ever after together. So, bearing this in mind I hit accept on a reasonably decent profile.

Ten minutes later I received a message from my reasonably decent gentleman. He got straight to the point and asked if I'd like to meet up? Spontaneity has always impressed me so I replied straightaway with a yes.

A few more messages bounced back and forth during the evening, ending with our confirmed date for the very next day. I went to sleep that night feeling slightly optimistic.

I woke fairly early on the day of my date, although we had arranged to meet up at lunch time, I wanted to spend a bit of time to prepare myself. Not knowing what to expect I prepared accordingly; full body scrub shower, hair wash and blow dry, neatly shaved legs, trimmed bikini line, matching underwear, easily removable outfit and classy high-heels. "Jeez Nicci, you're meeting for coffee not full-blown sex" I said out loud looking into the mirror. But I had always believed in; if you feel good you present good.

Showering my usual hugs on Milo and reassuring my mum that 'no I would not do anything stupid' I set off to meet my date.

I scanned the customers in the coffee shop and couldn't see my date, although, he could be here as his profile had displayed only one photograph and I couldn't remember what he looked like. But, feeling fairly confident he wasn't here already, I sat at a table in the window to wait. After about ten minutes I telephoned Pip, just to check in. Whilst chatting to Pip I noticed a man across the café who did look a little bit like my date; but decided it couldn't be him as he was looking right past me. Then as I put my phone down, he walked towards me, smiling, and said "Hi, Nicci?" whilst still looking right past me. Upon closer inspection it appeared he had a lazy eye.

We ordered our coffees and made our introductions. I noticed his hands shook quite badly, as he emptied six sugar sachets into his cup, possibly only stopping as there wasn't a seventh. I had also noticed his teeth were in terrible condition and wondered if this was a result of his excessive sugar intake?

We made the usual small talk, asking how much success each had with this online dating saga and both declaring online dating sucks. When he asked me where I lived, I told a small white lie and said I lived with my mother. Somehow saying out loud I lived in a van, with a dog, in my mother's back garden sounded a bit trampy. But on reflection, a nearing fifty-year-old woman living with her mother didn't sound much better.

Our conversation was pleasant enough, there were no long silences, and I'd got quite used to his lazy eye and stopped wondering what was behind me. His nerves seemed to have settled and his hands shook less often as he sipped his sweet coffee. We ordered a second coffee, chatted some more and then motioned for the bill, which we split down the middle and I was grateful they didn't charge for sugar. We then left the café with my date insisting he walk me to my car.

As I approached my car, I saw a homeless man sat in a doorway "Any spare change, love?" He asked me politely. As I rooted in my handbag, I heard my date huff and then say "If he got himself a job he wouldn't have to beg for money".

"I don't think it's quite that simple" I said, quite taken aback by his remark. "He doesn't have anywhere to live".

"Well if he actually got a job he could then find somewhere to live" My date further huffed.

Shocked by his ignorance, I handed my coins to the homeless man, who even though appearing extremely cold and uncomfortable, was still able to afford me a big smile and a gracious thank you.

"Some people aren't fortunate enough to own a motor-home and live in their mums back garden" I told my date, quite indignantly.

He looked at me blankly and as I looked down at him, standing a fair few inches shorter than me, I thought to myself, stick to your list, Nicci. I walked away, without saying goodbye, and drove off; back to the luxury of my own home.

Back in my van Mum popped in and enquired about my date.

"I met a cross-eyed dwarf, with bad teeth and a mis-held belief that life is easy" I told my mum.

"Oh, no second date then?" She replied.

We went to that place I love and hate today. I love it because all the shelves are adorned with bags of food. I hate it because it is a Veterinary Surgery. I remember our last visit here, I left wearing, what I can only describe as, a lampshade around my neck. And the mean man wrapped some tasty looking cloth around my paw, which, try as I might I just couldn't reach, what with that stupid lampshade round my neck.

It was the same mean man today. So, I jumped on the chair and tried to hide behind Mee. But she stood up and walked towards the mean man. I therefore had to follow her, so, placing my front paws on her shoulders I walked behind her on my two back paws. I was hoping the mean man hadn't seen me but on entering another room he lifted me off her and made me sit on the floor beside her. Then he waffled on for ages talking about; worms: rabies: ticks and fleas. He popped something into my mouth, which I know for a fact did not come from one of those tasty bags I saw when we arrived, but I swallowed it anyway, and then we left. Mee was grumping on about something to do with money, I was just happy not to be wearing a lampshade.

Chapter 4

With only about a week before my departure date, I was still a little fearful but also beginning to feel excited. I'd recently done a few radio interviews including Radio Scotland, BBC 5 Live and an interview with Derek Mooney on RTE radio. He kindly invited me to the studio in Dublin, to do a follow up interview on my arrival. The interview with Derek Mooney was good fun and full of banter, although I had struggled to understand his strong Irish accent.

I'd also received an early birthday present, in the post, from my best friend Sue. A fiftieth birthday present. Yikes! I would turn fifty in May. The big five 'O'. Maybe, I hoped, I would be spending my fiftieth birthday with the man of my dreams, in a romantic location somewhere in Ireland? I was most impressed that Sue believed in me; believed that I would still be travelling by May and not locked up in some Thai prison! I also received, from Pip and her boyfriend, an SJCAM for my birthday. This tiny camera would hopefully capture some amazing footage of my adventure. Pip also had the foresight to buy me a new sat-nav, the one I'd used in Scotland constantly failed me, so hopefully this one would keep me on the right road. I personally chose to indulge in the purchase of a pair of mini binoculars, something I regretted not having in Scotland.

Visiting local charity shops, I now had a good selection of books to read, mainly being my usual choice of gruesome murder mysteries. For evening entertainment, other than my books, I only had my Netflix account; because I still couldn't figure out how to operate my TV. Mind you I usually only logged into Netflix to answer the question "who's watching?" And I got to answer, "Mum". Just a little reminder of who I was, and I also loved the fact that my son was paying for the account.

The Beast had been given a thorough clean on the outside. I'd spent a good few hours with a bucket of hot, soapy water and my mum's soft garden brush, giving him a good scrub down. Milo observed this activity, excitedly bouncing from window to window, chasing the brush, from inside the van.

Getting the Beast out of my mum's back garden was even harder than getting it in. Luckily, I'd ticked the engine over regularly, so it started first time. But having removed the gate and fence panel I now had to reverse out into the road, avoiding the lamp post on one side and mum's garage on the other. It was not easy. I had Pip's boyfriend guiding me with unseen hand gestures and instructions of "Hard left!" "Hard right!" all to be performed without power steering. Having had to pull in my wing mirror's I had no view at all and may as well have closed my eyes. With the added obstacle of a small ridge to reverse over, the Beast was struggling. At one point we really thought it wasn't going to happen. I had literally millimetres either side and was trying to decide whether Mum would be angrier at me knocking down the lamp post or the corner of her garage. But somehow, I got out, without a scratch.

The Beast was free and I headed up to my local Wirral Small Cars where my friend, Paul was to give him some well-earned TLC, before our departure tomorrow. This confused Milo immensely. Having lived in the van for months, Milo watched me, from Mum's window, drive off up the road without him. I don't know whether he thought "Thank God, she's gone." Or "She forgot to take me." Anyway, I was only gone about an hour and he seemed pleased to see me when I got back.

Tonight, I was having my last bubbly bath in my mum's. Yet again I was going to miss this activity the most. But on a good note, Philip had informed me he would   be in Dublin around the week of my birthday on a business trip. He suggested, if I wasn't too far away, we could meet up for a meal. I had in mind that instead of a meal, I could have a bath at his hotel.

So, tomorrow was D-Day. No more being wrapped in cotton wool. No tapping on my mum's back door if I ran out of milk. No regular use of her free washing machine. No more safely cocooned between a house and a garage. It was the open road once again for Milo, Me and the Beast. Another adventure. Another journey. This time it would work, I would meet the man of my dreams and I would live happily ever after.

I had a moment of panic today. There seemed to be much commotion in her mother's yard and I was placed in the house whilst they removed part of the fence. I didn't mind being in her mother's house as this got me closer to her food supply, but I was curious as to what they were up to outside. Then I heard them all cheer and I ran to the window and saw Mee disappear up the road in our Beast. Well I barked and I barked, I barked my loudest bark ever. The sister came in the house and said "hey, don't worry, she'll be back soon" Huh! Last time they said that she was gone ages. But sure enough she was back within the hour telling me all was good, the Beast had been to a doctor and was fit to travel. Well let's just hope this doctor hasn't made him wear one of those stupid lampshades!

Milo, Me and The Beast in Mum's back garden

Chapter 5

The night before our ferry to Dublin we parked up on the promenade beside the River Mersey in Liverpool. With such an early morning ferry departure, it made sense to be nearby. After a nice pub meal with my family and the usual hugs and kisses goodbye, I headed back to the Beast. Milo seemed unsettled and chose to sleep on the driver's seat all night. In the morning after a good run about on the promenade we headed to the ferry terminal to set sail for Dublin.

I approached the check-in booth, wound down the window and presented my documents.

"Good morning, Love, how many travelling?" Enquired the friendly man.

"Just me and Milo." I replied.

"OK, Love. We just need to check inside your motor-home, if you can just open your back door please." He said.

Unlocking the back door, a big, burly policeman stepped inside the van. Of course, this set Milo into killer dog overdrive. He bounced from couch to couch, raising his head as high as he could to make his bark even more threatening. The burly policeman just laughed, patted Milo's head and said in his strong Scouse accent: "Arrh Ay, your dog's boss."

We were told to park in a bay near the check-in booth, until we were instructed to board the ferry. We seemed to be waiting for ages, so I put on some tunes and tried to figure out how to set up the dash cam to film our boarding. Whilst doing this a white Bedford van parked up beside us. I turned to look, and the driver shot me a big smile. I returned the smile.

"Where you off to, Gorgeous?" He shouted through his window.

"We're touring the coast." I replied.

"We?" He questioned. "You got a big hunky fella asleep in that bunk?"

"Oh, no." I answered. "Just me and my Milo." I said pointing at Milo on the passenger seat beside me.

"How's about I book us a cabin and we have ourselves a 'passionate' crossing, Eh, sexy?"

"Er, no thanks." I politely replied and quickly wound up my window.

A good start or a bad start to our journey, I wondered, as I felt his eyes boring into my back.

I could now see all the cars starting to board the ferry. It seemed, I was to be the last vehicle to board. As I approached the steep ramp up to the hull of the ship the Beast struggled, I gave him a bit of rev as the man in the high-vis vest waved me towards him. He then started waving some other hand instructions of which I could not understand. He approached my window and said, "Just turn around and come back in reverse, against the side of the hull as tight as you can love."

Reverse? Yikes! he said reverse. Just like that. Reverse up-hill, over a ramp, onto a ship, into a rather small space beside a massive lorry, and all with no power steering. Yes, I can do this, I told myself. Adopt 'trucker mode' and you can do it Nicci, I decided. And I did. I swung onto that ship like a true trucker.

Feeling rather proud of my driving skills boarding the ferry I couldn't wait to view my dash-cam footage. Unfortunately, I'd pressed pause instead of record and had no evidence whatsoever.

Milo was not allowed out of the motor-home whilst at sea. My instruction leaflet stated; if escorted by a staff member, I would be allowed to visit him during the crossing.

"Hey, Baby. I'm just going to the shops." I lied.

"I won't be long." I continued to lie. "You be a good boy and I'll see you later."

Milo looked terrified. The noises coming from the ship were likely spooking him. I felt so guilty leaving him but at least he was in his 'home' I consoled myself. I popped him a biscuit, grabbed my bag and headed up to the passenger area.

I was most impressed with P&O Ferries; my ticket included a complimentary breakfast and unlimited free coffee. Once I'd finished my breakfast, having saved a couple of sausages for Milo, I grabbed my coffee to go and find a seat. And, immediately saw 'Mr Passion' grinning from ear to ear when he spotted me. I quickly diverted my gaze and headed in the opposite direction.

Having found a member of staff and visited Milo with my left-over breakfast, I now stood on deck as we approached the port of Dublin. Excitement filled me, the sun was shining, and I could already see a beach in the distance. This was going to be fine, I decided. Ireland, The Emerald Isle. Let our adventure begin.

'Shops' She must think I'm daft. I'm in the hull of a ship, alone, scared and abandoned. Okay, not quite true; I'm tucked up in my blanket, safe inside the Beast, being lulled into a blissful sleep with a comforting rocking sensation, but I had to give her my sad Labrador look when she left for the 'shops' to ensure the promise of biscuits. She did seem to take quite a while to return, at one point I thought she might have taken up that offer of 'passion' from the gorilla. But, true to her word, she returned, clutching a napkin, stuffed with sausages and bacon and showered me with an abundance of her loving hugs.

Chapter 6

The first thing I did when leaving Dublin ferry terminal was take a wrong turn. This resulted in me paying a road toll, twice. I was heading for a camp-site I'd booked on-line which was apparently very close to the port. About an hour later than anticipated we arrived at our camp-site in a place called Rush and pitched up. After a good few hours spent frolicking on the beach, we both slept well.

The next day, a taxi picked me up from the camp-site and took me to the RTE studio, in Dublin city centre. Here, I had the pleasure of doing a radio interview with the lovely Ray Darcy. Everyone there was so lovely to me and they all made me feel quite welcome. Ray Darcy did question whether I was in fact brave or mad for going on this adventure. I couldn't answer that. I just hoped that maybe, somebody listening, would save me from this madness I'd created.

Back at the camp-site, Milo was most pleased to see me and immediately insisted we go back to the beach. Later that evening I decided to use the camp-site shower facilities. A lot of camp-sites charge you to use their showers, even though you have already paid to pitch up. I placed my two-euro coin in the slot, not realising this immediately turned on the shower. So, quick as I could, I ripped off all my clothes and jumped under the water before my coin ran out. It was possibly the quickest shower I've ever had as I only had one coin. But at least it was hot.

We left Rush, stopping overnight in Dunbar Upper. This camp-site was basically just a field on a cliff, but it was cheap. The views were stunning, and our location was so peaceful, but unfortunately, I'd parked on a steep incline. Rather than go through the whole process to unhook and re-pitch, I chose to spend the entire night with a 'lean forward feeling'. Every time I placed my mug of coffee on my table top it slid towards me.

I got quite lost again the next day. I was heading for Dungarvan and somehow went via Carlow. I did wonder if I would ever make sense of my sat-nav. I think I was taking her instructions too literally, so, if she said turn left, I immediately did, even if it was someone's driveway. Anyway, I got to see more locations than intended so I didn't mind. Not sure how the residents of Ireland felt though.

Our camp-site in Dungarvan was a huge error on my part. I hadn't checked the price on-line and was charged thirty-eight euros for one night. Shower facilities were also charged as an extra. The camp-site was constructed of mainly concrete, with all the vans parked far too close together for my liking. There was no sandy beach within walking distance, only a very rocky one, covered in seaweed. I am scared of seaweed. I have been scared of seaweed ever since I was a small child. I believe seaweed can bite you.

To make matters worse, back at the van, I threw the ball for Milo and when he jumped up to catch it, he scratched his face on the side of the Beast. He was now sporting a badly cut eye. Not a good look, especially so as we were doing a TV interview the day after tomorrow in Cork.

The next morning, I reluctantly headed to 'cell block H' for my shower. With hindsight I took two coins with me. A good call on my part because the 'prison block shower' took so long to heat up it switched off mid hair wash. My second coin was much appreciated.

We happily left our camp-site and headed towards Ballycotton, to meet up with Patricia, a lady I'd befriended on Twitter.

Well I wasn't too impressed with that camp-site. Far too much concrete and not enough grass for my liking. We did venture on to the beach but it was awfully rocky and Mee kept squealing out-loud every-time she saw a piece of seaweed, I had a piece stuck in my collar at one point and she couldn't even touch it – insisted on using the ball chucker to try and remove it. I can't really take the mick out of her 'fears' because my list of fears is so much longer than hers; the dark, aeroplanes, hair-dryers, Hoovers, lawnmowers, guns. To be honest anything that makes a loud noise scares me, especially in the dark. Although, I am quite adept at disguising this fear; by jumping up and down on all four paws and barking ferociously at anything that scares me.

Chapter 7

We arrived in Ballycotton late afternoon. Having sent an SOS message to Patricia she was now standing in the road outside her house, because I had passed it twice already. She waved us in and guided the Beast onto the drive next to her house.

Patricia worked for the Guide Dog association and had been following my blog with interest.

"Oh, Nicci. It's so lovely to meet you in person." Said Patricia, in her soft Irish accent.

"Come into the house, bring Milo."

And then, from her house, out bounced Nemo, her ever so friendly Labrador. Milo then shot straight back into the van and refused to come out. Inside Patricia's house we sat at the kitchen table with a pot of hot coffee. I filled her in on my journey so far and told her of my TV interview tomorrow. Patricia told me she had just that minute telephoned her husband, Kieron, asking him to pick up a bottle of wine on his way home from work, for our 'house guest'.

"Erm, what 'house guest'?" Kieron had inquired.

"Oh, just a woman and her dog, I found them on Twitter. They are travelling Ireland in a motor-home looking for a husband." She casually told him.

"And you thought you would just invite this random woman and her dog to stay in our home?" Asked Kieron, quite bemused.

Luckily, like me, Patricia had a good judge of character. Patricia and Kieron were just the loveliest couple. They fed me up with a home cooked meal then took me to their local pub, The Blackbird, where we listened to live music and I was introduced to all their friends and had a fun filled evening, full of Irish banter.

The next morning, they left for work early, insisting I have the full run of their house and to just shut the door when leaving. I was quite overwhelmed by their kindness.

Rather than take the Beast into Cork city centre, Patricia and Kieron had told me of a large park and ride car-park on the outskirts of the city. We headed there, having arranged with the TV company to be collected here and taken by a taxi to the studio.

Milo and I arrived at the RTE TV studio and introduced ourselves at reception. We were then instructed to take a seat whilst the receptionist went off to find someone to take us upstairs. Just as she disappeared through the door I, stupidly, let go of Milo's lead and he immediately dived behind the reception desk and got stuck into a box of cup-cakes. I managed to pull him away just before the receptionist returned, noting he had only eaten one cake, and silently hoping she may not notice.

Upstairs, in the Green Room, there was a spread laid out on the table of various refreshments. Milo went straight for the plate of biscuits. Having moved them to a higher shelf we settled down on the couch to wait for our interview. Three hours later we were still sitting in the Green Room. Milo was completely frustrated, bearing in mind he had seen where I'd put the biscuits, and I was pretty fed up too. Apparently, Pip was watching the show, live, back in England and could hear Milo barking in the background.

Eventually it was our turn to head to the studio for our interview with Daithi and Maura. The cameras were rolling, and we were sat on the big red couch being introduced. But as the camera panned on us Milo was climbing over the back of the couch, whilst I had my backside on view trying to haul him back. Milo was more than keen to get off that couch for most of the interview and find out what that smell was; coming from the kitchen set beside us. I spent most of the interview gripping Milo's lead and trying to stop him from dragging me with him towards whatever was being cooked in the kitchen. I've still to this day not seen this interview but Pip told me Milo stole the show.

After a very long day it was far too late to drive to the camp-site I had planned on. But the kind receptionist, obviously having not noticed her missing cup-cake, telephoned the local airport hotel and asked if we would be allowed to park up overnight in their secure car-park, in the Beast. The hotel manager kindly agreed to this, although I was slightly disappointed that he didn't offer us a complimentary hotel room.

It wasn't a great night's sleep. Milo is terrified of the sound of aeroplanes. Every time one took off or landed, he would hide, quivering under the driver seat. He spent all night under that seat which must have been quite uncomfortable for him. We left our 'runway' spot early and drove to the beach at Garrettstown, this soon cheered Milo up. We spent all day on the beach, choosing to wild camp there that night. In the morning I stood at my back door brushing my teeth and could feel the spray from the incoming tide on my face, the sun was rising and there wasn't a soul in sight. Wild camping at its best.

Later that day we checked into a very quiet camp-site in Timoleague. Our only neighbours were two resident sheepdogs who insisted on trying to steal Milo's ball. They sat barking at our back door and then followed us on our entire walk, even trying to take the ball from Milo's mouth. We eventually gave up on our walk and retreated back to the van, where the sheepdogs chose to sit at our door in wait. Later in the day, when the sheepdogs had given up waiting, we trotted over to the on-site laundry room, filled up the machine, popped in a few euros and hit start. Nothing. After much button pushing, plug checking and now quite a few euros down, I gave up and headed over to the owner's house. I knocked on the front door and waited. And waited. I knocked again and still waited. The porch door was ajar so I stuck my head in and shouted "anybody home?". No answer. Hmm I thought "what are we going to do now Milo?" "Milo?" He was nowhere to be seen. He had been standing right beside me when I first knocked on the door, now I couldn't see him anywhere. I wandered round to the side of the house and there he was, in the open garage with his head deep into a large sack of dog food. I grabbed his collar, pulled his head out of the sack and retreated back to the Beast, stopping en-route to kick the washing machine, which seemed to do the trick.

Blooming sheepdogs! They think they're so superior with all their sheep gathering skills. Well they're not so clever at catching a ball, oh no, that skill belongs to me. Top marks for their persistence though, I thought they'd never leave. We even had to cut short our walk as Mee got fed up with them jumping up at her trying to grab 'my' ball. We sat in the Beast for ages, waiting for them to leave. I tried a bit of my growl-barking but they still hung around. It was quite late in the day before we ventured outside again and then Bam! Bonus! I found, quite by accident, their food supply. I was having a little wander around the premises, while Mee was loitering at a door, and there it was. A massive, opened sack, full to the brim with biscuits. It had my name written all over it, so I grabbed the opportunity and dived right in. I could have quite easily finished that whole sack if Mee hadn't grabbed me by the collar and dragged me off. Well, that'll teach those sneaky sheepdogs for trying to steal my ball.

Chapter 8

We spent the next few days either on camp-sites or wild camping. Our scenery was stunning, and our beaches were breath-taking. One of our over-nights we spent at a Safe Night Ireland I had booked in Roscarberry. This was a private house that looked just like a Battenberg cake, all pink and pretty. The very friendly lady of the house gave us use of her internet whilst parked on her drive. The next day, leaving Roscarberry, I got slightly lost again and ended up in a place called Union Hall. I took the opportunity to make use of a local pub, with free internet. I sat by the log burning fire and settled down to re-map my journey. Looking around my surroundings I spotted a little placard on the wall which made me giggle: Wanted – a good woman who can clean, sew, cook, fish, dig worms and owns boat and motor – send photo of boat and motor. I reckon I had nearly everything going for me, other than owning a boat. Whilst enjoying my coffee, I got talking to a local gentleman seated at the next table, who very kindly gave me a list of places to visit, insisting if I mentioned his name it would go down rather well. Unfortunately, ten minutes down the road I had forgotten his name.

I was now in Skiberdeen and having stopped at the local Aldi, I was now driving towards Baltimore. As I was exiting the Aldi car-park I saw a young girl on the side of the road hitch hiking. Why not? I thought and indicated to pull over.

Roisin was her name. She had been in Cork for the weekend and having bused as far as she could, she was now hitching to Baltimore, to catch the ferry over to Sherkin Island, where she lived. We merrily chatted away on the route, and I told her all about my adventure.

"Would you like to stop in the bushes before I board my ferry?" Roisin asked me.

Weird, I thought. Must be some kind of local Irish thing. Roisin could see the look of confusion on my face and laughed out loud.

"The Bushie is a pub on the harbour." She laughed.

"I can buy you a drink to thank you for the lift, Milo too." She said.

"Oh lovely, thank you, Roisin." I replied, feeling quite relieved.

We parked up near the harbour and walked down to the Bushie pub. And here I had my first glass of Murphy's, recommended by Roisin. It was quite delicious. Then Roisin took me to meet her friend Mark. He lived in a cottage just up the road. Milo was most impressed as Mark was eating a fried egg sandwich and gave him the crusts. We stayed at Marks for about an hour, he recommended some safe places nearby for me to park overnight. Then I walked back to the harbour with Roisin, where she boarded her ferry. Roisin insisted Milo and I visit her on Sherkin Island, she told us to pop over any time tomorrow and head to the Jolly Roger pub, the place where she worked and lived.

Sherkin Island is a little oasis, an island with a population of about 100 people. Milo was extremely well behaved on the ferry, which only took about ten minutes from Baltimore harbour. We spent most of the day walking most of the island. I don't think we saw another human being all day. At one beach I found a comfy spot in the sand and lay back for a little snooze with Milo, it was so peaceful. The only sounds were 'natural' sounds; birds, waves, the wind in the trees. Not an ounce of 'white noise'. Later in the day we found The Jolly Roger pub and had a drink with Roisin. I can quite understand why she loves living here.

We spent two nights wild camping at the harbour in Baltimore and then continued our journey following the coast roads. Unfortunately, over the next few days I became quite ill. My whole body ached, and I had no energy. I was feeling so sorry for myself. Milo, my little star, seemed to pick up on my mood; he was extremely well behaved. But everyday things were becoming so difficult for me. Even just driving the Beast was such an effort, with no power steering the winding roads were so strenuous on my body.

We'd stopped at Mizen Head and as the car-park was completely empty, we chose to stay there overnight. I decided this would be a good opportunity to attach my mini video camera to Milo's collar. The views from the cliff top were spectacular and I thought if I threw his ball into the field the camera would pick up the amazing scenery on his run to fetch it. I could then upload this incredible footage to YouTube and people would surely pay to view it? What a marvellous idea I thought, as Milo sat very still, whilst I attached the camera to his collar.

"Ready, camera, action!" I shouted to Milo.

And I pulled back the ball chucker ready to launch the ball into the field. Unfortunately, my aim was slightly misguided and I chucked the ball right into the middle of the car-park. Milo did his usual and ran in the direction he thought the ball was being aimed, and then did an abrupt U-turn to chase it across the car-park. At this point, the little camera slid around his neck and landed just under his chin. My 'incredible' footage consisted of two long minutes of grey concrete and the sound of Milo's heavy panting.

This was also the night my kitchen sink blocked and chose to rise up the pipe and into my shower tray.

In my ignorance I decided boiling water would solve this blockage. With a plunger in one hand and a kettle of boiled water in the other, I poured and plunged in a somewhat vigorous manner. As the unsightly mess of brown gunge bubbled up into the shower tray I woefully regretted spending all those weeks pouring my coffee grains down the sink. The more water I poured down the kitchen sink, the more the brown gunk came up into the shower tray. Dismayed, I stepped back to observe what now looked like a sewer in front of me. Unfortunately, as I stepped back, I lost my grip of the kettle and screamed out loud as the boiling water splattered down my legs. Jumping up and down, screaming like a mad woman, I desperately tried to pull my skinny jeans away from my scalding skin beneath. Milo lay very still on the couch, one eye open, watching this whole charade.

The shower tray was not draining; this, I conceded, meant I would have to go outside, in the dark and crawl under the van to disconnect the main drain pipe from the waste water tank. Ten minutes later, I crawled back into the van, battered and bruised and covered from head to toe in the gunge from the pipe. I cried myself to sleep that night.

I did not sleep well and I had a horrible dream which really spooked me out; Earlier in the day I had come across a placard, situated on the cliff top. I read the story, engraved upon the placard, telling the tragic tale of a shipwreck below the cliffs of Mizen Head, many years ago. Hundreds of survivors were found, by local villagers, crawling up the cliffs of Mizen Head, and sadly, the only female onboard had been crushed to death by the lifeboat; In my nightmare I could hear a tapping on my van window and cautiously climbed out of my bed to open the curtain. And there, at my window, was the crushed female from the ship wreck, staring right into my soul. I think my own screams woke me from this nightmare and no doubt Milo too.

The next day, we left Mizen Head and stopped in Crookhaven to purchase some drain clearing fluid. Whilst here, a journalist from The Clare Champion newspaper telephoned me for an interview. One question she asked me was "Nicci, what do you desire from a man?" "The state I'm in at the moment, poor eyesight would be good!" I replied.

Leaving Crookhaven I got lost again and whilst trying to read a road sign I hit a brick wall: literally. A good description of how I felt at that moment 'hitting a brick wall'; Feeling utterly exhausted and so unwell, with a blocked drain and a substantial chunk missing from the side of the Beast: I really felt like giving up that day...

I think she lost the plot last night. She cried, she cursed and at one point she was even dancing. Then she went outside and came back crying even more and stinking of goodness knows what. I heard her crying into her pillow later, I know she was trying to muffle it but my hearing is impeccable. Mee thinks I don't understand, but I do. She can say nothing, but I see it in her eyes. I know she is scared, I know she is determined. Put these two together and she is now exhausted. Burn out I think they call it. I wish I could help more. She's set herself quite a challenge 'finding a husband' she can't even find her keys half the time!

Chapter 9

I made the right decision to 'not to give up' and booked into the Hungry Hill camp-site near the Healy Pass. After having two, glorious hot showers and hanging my washing on my own private washing line, I was beginning to feel human again. There's no better feeling than beginning to feel better after an illness. I was lying on the couch with Milo reflecting on my journey so far.

I'd seen some stunning scenery, I'd met some lovely people and I was living my life exactly how I wanted to. I was still experiencing down moments, but they felt different now. They weren't my previous dark black clouds, weighing down on me and consuming all my thoughts with fears of no solution. Now I just had incidentals, hiccups I could rationalise and correct. This adventure was providing a calm and non-chaotic lifestyle, well, mainly. Life was simple: eat; sleep; travel. All I needed in life, was inside of my Beast; Milo, Me and a few precious possessions. We would continue to take one day at a time on our adventure.

We left the Hungry Hill camp-site feeling quite refreshed and travelled on, over the Healy Pass. We only saw one other car on the road, but saw plenty sheep on the way. The rugged scenery was breath-taking and even Milo sat with his head hanging out the window taking in the views. I pulled over and parked up to take a photograph looking back up at the long and winding road. Milo jumped into the driver's seat and looked quite the part steering the Beast.

Derrynane was our next stop. A beautiful bay that afforded us a beach on either side of our motor-home. We spent all day exploring the rock coves on the beaches and wild-camped that night under a sky so black and yet so illuminated with stars - there was little light pollution in this part of the world. The next morning, I was privy to a lovely little sight; I was sat in my conservatory, cup of coffee in hand, and watching through my binoculars, in the distance, a little old man, carrying a posy of pink flowers; he crossed the beach and slowly climbed up the hill to the little cemetery at the top. There, he stopped beside a grave, actioned the cross sign, and slowly bent down to place the posy against the head stone. He was there for a long time, often looking out to sea, often rubbing his eyes beneath his spectacles. I like to think he was visiting his wife, with whom he'd had a long and loving marriage and had been blessed with adoring children. He would be praying for the day he could be a permanent visitor - because death is not always so bad.

In fact, death in Ireland is not a taboo subject, it is a big business. Many a time my radio would only tune into hours of death notices being broadcast. In Ireland, talking about death is a conversation, there is a morbid fascination with it. There are only two certainties in life; we're born and we die. In Ireland, you're only as good as your last funeral.

We left our secluded beach spot and drove to Inch beach, which was quite different in comparison. Miles and miles of open stretch sand, cars and people everywhere. We parked up on the beach, beside various other motor-homes and spent the day people watching, reading and generally just chilling. That is until, late into the evening, when I realised I was the only vehicle left parked on the beach.

"Hey Milo we've got the whole beach to ourselves" I declared.

Milo had his head on the dashboard and let out a long, low snort from his nose. I looked out the window and saw the tide coming in towards us. It was still a fair distance from our van, but I had no idea how close it would come. I looked out the side windows to see if the debris in the sand could give me any clues. It did appear that we were parked far enough back not to be carried away, to a distant land, by a large and imposing wave. But I couldn't be sure. Why was nobody else parked here? If it was that safe then surely there would be tons of other people camping? I decided not to take the chance, started up the engine and headed off the beach to look for a safer place to sleep. Safer proved to be dismal. After driving miles with darkness approaching and my eyes getting heavy, I pulled into some waste ground and switched off the engine. Then I lit up like a rabbit in headlights. I was parked on an S bend and cars from both directions were approaching with full beam headlights shooting right into my face. I was just far too tired to move, so pulled shut the curtains, curled under a blanket and fell asleep.

It was now early morning and I was driving towards Dingle. I had received, through social media, an invitation to stay with Janet and Seamus on their sheep farm. After a few wrong turns we eventually arrived at their home to a most auspicious welcome. Janet guided us, as I reversed the Beast into a neat little corner beside a field brimming with bouncing, new born lambs. Unfortunately, Milo was not allowed out of the van if the sheepdogs were outside. These were professional sheepdogs and had a real job to do, Milo bouncing around and barking would certainly interfere with their work. Not all bad though, I put Milo's lead on him and headed up the lanes for a walk, where Milo was quite happy to eat all the sheep droppings.

Janet was of American descent and had lived here for many years. Seamus was local, born and bred. They made me feel most welcome and I took full advantage of the hot shower on offer.

Later in the evening, Janet and Seamus took me to a local pub, where Janet was performing. There was live music all night, and Janet was pretty amazing on her harmonica. There also seemed to be some kind of private celebration going on and I just happened to be sitting right beside the buffet table. I don't think anyone saw me stuffing a handful of sausage rolls into my handbag for Milo.

The next day Janet took me into Dingle harbour, I had a good wander around and although I didn't manage to see Fungie, the Dolphin I did manage to sample the renowned Murphy's ice-cream. I met up with Janet later in a quaint little pub called Dick Macks where she was playing her harmonica. This pub appeared to have never changed since time began. One side homed the original shop counter, still displaying items for sale from years gone by, there were shoes, books and even old chamber pots. The other side homed the bar, backdropped by the largest display of whiskies I'd ever seen, the barman handed me a whisky drinks menu, which was basically a book, I stuck to Guinness. Many of the pubs in Dingle still housed the original ladies only snug, and all of them held an abundance of character with memories of past lives.

Back at the van, after a Milo walk, Seamus invited me to accompany him on a sheep check. We drove to the top of the mountain behind his house and parked up near a small tumbled down cottage. Inside were some sheep, ready to give birth imminently. Seamus then gave me a quick lesson on how to herd the rest of the sheep into an adjoining field, this entailed a bit of shouting and a lot of arm waving, I thought I was pretty good at it. I also got to meet the Daddy sheep; he was a big, strong looking fella and, quite rightly so, looked rather proud of his achievements. Back in the barn, I was allowed to bottle feed the new-borns, from a beer bottle, teated and full of milk. They were so cute and cuddly that I decided there and then, that I would not eat roast, minted lamb again; until this memory had left me.

We spent a few wonderful days on the sheep farm and then spent an even more wonderful night, wild camping, just down the road at Clogher Head. The sight and sound of the Atlantic waves crashing against the rugged rocks mesmorised me, it was like watching avalanches of snow landing in the ocean. Milo was obviously aware of how treacherous this water was, because even though he loved to swim, he always kept his distance from the shore line. We had the whole of little bay to ourselves, except for when a mini bus turned up and the occupants sat on the beach for an hour singing and dancing to some local Irish tunes; all quite entertaining. I even had a view, in the distance, of a mountain top, where they were filming the next Star Wars movie, sadly there were no hunky American movie stars knocking on the Beast's door that night. Although, I did have a visit from a gang of local boy racers.

At about 2am I awoke to the sound of gravel being sprayed all over the side of my van. Hearing the roars of engines and the screech of tyres as they continuously spun their cars in circles, I lay completely still in my bunk, too terrified to breathe let alone move. The inside of my van lit up with the glare from their headlights and I could see Milo's little eyes looking up at me from his couch below. Normally Milo would bark at anything, but it seemed even he was too scared to move. The cars continued to spin, horns blazing and voices shouting. Scenarios of what 'could happen' filled my head as I fumbled under my pillow to locate my phone. My fear amplified as I saw my mobile phone display the dreaded 'No Service' sign on the screen. This is it, I thought, the end of Milo and Me, a gruesome, grisly end. So, I pulled the duvet up over my head, curled into a ball and held my breath. And miraculously woke up in the morning alive and well.

Another update of our story had been printed, this time in The Irish Examiner newspaper, and I had received many more friendly messages on social media. The trouble was, whenever I got a decent invitation to visit someone it was usually after I had left that particular area. Maybe I should slow down, I thought? But somehow, I always felt the need to keep moving, like I was trying to reach somewhere, but I didn't know where.

The next few days were another mixture of camp-sites and wild camping. Curragh Chase Forest was a favourite spot, we spent two nights in a peaceful camping site and were surrounded by nothing but trees. I didn't want to leave, but this is where my gas bottle ran out and I had such trouble replacing it. Apparently, my gas bottle was an 'English' model and I ended up having to drive into Limerick city centre to purchase a replacement.

That night, having been ripped off for a gas bottle, we booked into Strandcamping in Doonbeg, a pristine camp site run by such a friendly lady. Three nights for the price of two - so we chose to stop for the three. Our next-door neighbours were two pleasant ladies travelling with their black and white cat. Well, they did have a cat, that is until Milo spotted it and chased it over the hedge, through a ditch and into the field beyond. I was assured it would return eventually.

That evening, I had arranged to meet up with Ciara from Ireland AM TV3. It was a television interview about my travels with Milo, looking for love. I drove the Beast into the local town and parked up, leaving Milo inside the van. I was meeting Ciara and her cameraman in a local hotel.

"Nicci, how lovely to meet you" Ciara enthused on my arrival.

She introduced me to the cameraman, who I must say was a rather handsome Spanish man, unfortunately too young and too married for me. Ciara then suggested we head down to the beach to do the interview.

"Why do you feel you've not met the man of your dreams so far, Nicci?" Ciara asked as we walked across the sand in front of the camera.

As my high heeled suede boots sank into the wet sand and the wind swept my rain-soaked hair all over my face, I stared across the deserted beach and said "I'm doing something wrong, Ciara". She laughed at my reply and suggested we should head to one of the local pubs to continue the interview.

Ciara decided she would travel with me in the Beast, to the pub, and beckoned the camera-man to film her on entering the van. The minute she opened the door Milo bounced onto the seat and went into his killer-dog-bark mode. Ciara literally screamed out loud and immediately banged the door shut. "How to win friends and influence people, Milo" I said under my breath. I think he was just spooked by the big camera and boom mic.

The pub proved to be as unsuccessful as the beach. Basically, two customers filled the bar area and the landlord suggested we should return tomorrow, when it would be much busier as they had a bingo night planned. I headed back to the camp-site having made arrangements to meet Ciara here in the morning, for some more filming.

As I was putting my pyjamas on, I could hear the lady next door.

"Here, Kitty, Kitty, Kitty" she whispered, shaking a box of cat biscuits.

"Where are you, Kitty?" She continued into the night.

Milo stared at me with a guilty expression, I tutted at him, curled under the duvet and eventually fell asleep.

The next morning, Ciara and the cameraman arrived with a box full of croissants and I made a pot of hot coffee. We sat outside the van, with the croissants on a table in-between us and commenced with the interview. Unfortunately, midway through the interview Milo managed to grab one of the croissants and swallow it whole. The cameraman then had to realign his camera angle so as the continuity flowed, editing out the table with the missing croissant.

Late in the day, when the TV crew eventually left, I reflected on all the questions I'd been asked. 'What exactly are you hoping to find on this quest?' seemed to be the main question. Finding my true love, a husband for my happy ever after, was, it appeared, a lot to be looking for. Would I ever find this or even come close? Was I looking for too much? Was I trying too hard? Would it happen before my fiftieth birthday? Hmm.

I consoled myself with the fact that at least next door had finally found their cat.

I've had an interesting few days this week. There have certainly been plenty of beaches, which is the best bit for me on this adventure. Mee's mood seems to have picked up too, for a while there I thought she was ready to give up on this adventure. This 'man hunt' she is on is proving to be rather difficult for her. She can't find one. I wonder if I should tell her that trawling around in a motor-home, camping under the stars, on deserted beaches is possibly a contributing factor? I do worry sometimes: that I am not helping the situation. The signs are everywhere: No Dogs Allowed. I do hope she is not missing out, but, as she keeps telling me 'if they don't want you, they can't have me', then I'll assume neither of us are missing out.

Anyway, she has received some help from a television show this week. Once I got to know them, they seemed to be a friendly bunch, they even brought cake for me. They filmed her for two days, so hopefully someone watching will see what I see; a kind, beautiful and sincere human being, who just happens to be a little bit crazy at times.

Chapter 10

Our next stop found us on a camp-site in Doolin. Certainly a picturesque camp-site, but a bit too busy for my liking. Too many people, dogs, bikes, tents and motor-homes and all having oodles of family fun, which only made me feel lonely. This camp-site was not within walking distance of a shop and led me to use my emergency tin of ham for my supper. There were no complaints from Milo.

I'd stopped en-route to Doolin at the Rock Shop where I felt compelled to purchase a Wish Jar; a little glass jar with a scroll inside it, upon which you wrote down your wish list and it was guaranteed angels granted you your wishes. I sat down in the Beast, poured a glass of wine and wrote out my wish list; true love, health, happiness, wealth, good friends, laughter, great sex and straight teeth. Yet again I wondered if I was asking too much?

"What do you reckon, Milo? Am I wishing for too much?"

"I'm fairly confident that if I could meet a good-looking dentist, I could build the list from there", I deduced.

Milo lay on the couch, eyes closed and snoring loudly. Then my phone rang.

It was local man Willie Daly, the famous third generation, traditional Irish Matchmaker. Julie, a lovely lady I'd met on Facebook, had given him my number. He introduced himself to me, confirmed it was myself, then went headlong into a lot of chatter, much of which I could not understand. The gist of it was; he wanted to meet me tomorrow at his house where we would chat about matching me with a suitable gentleman, then Willie would take me to a horse fair in the nearby town of Ennistynon.

"I do have one particular gentleman available at the moment and his only request of a lady is; that her big toe is her biggest toe." Willie informed me.

I looked down at my bare feet and thought to myself, 'things are looking up'.

The next day, we fired up the Beast and headed to Willie's house. It was a rambling old property in a beautiful location. His land was vast and strewn with horses.

"Wow, how many horses do you have, Willie?" I asked, impressed with how many I saw.

"A man never counts his money, his wives or his horses." Willie answered, quite sincerely.

That afternoon the horse fair in Ennistynon was in full swing, a timeless tradition to behold. The town was a hive of activity, packed with people of all ages, some of them galloping horses bare-back up and down the high street. The pavements were strewn with cages housing various livestock for sale, even miniature ponies. There was a fair amount of bartering going on and even Willie added to his horse stock. Everybody knew Willie, everybody stopped to chat with him. It was an eye-opener of a day for Milo and me, I kept Milo on a tight leash, fearful he may be inadvertently sold.

Back at Willie's house, Milo tucked up in the van, Willie picked up his guitar and burst into song at the kitchen table. His songs were all stories of love and recited with a glint in his eye. After a few hours of singing we set off for a local Ceilidh dance, but not before I'd touched the Lucky Love Book on the kitchen table.

The next morning, I drove into the town of Lisdoonvarna and was given an education into its historical background. Julie had organised a private tour for me with local man, Pat, who passionately filled me in on the full history. Hundreds of years ago, people travelled from miles around to reap the healing benefits of the waters, rich in sulphur and iron. They would drink it and bathe in it, I personally drank some and bad eggs came to mind. Over the years, bachelor farmers would come to facilitate the spa in the autumn after harvest and their thoughts would often turn to finding a partner. A middle-man's skills would be required, hence the introduction of a matchmaker, like Willie Daly. Today, the Lisdoonvarna Matchmaking Festival takes place every year for the whole month of September. People come from all over the world for the music, the dancing and the craic. Willie Daly is ever present offering his skills to bring hopefuls together.

Willie must be doing something right as later that day I received quite a few interesting phone calls. To be honest I could hardly understand a word they were saying to me but they all seem to start their conversation with; "Hello, is it Mary?" "Are you a widow, Mary?" "Are you a Catholic, Mary?" I told them all 'I am neither a widow nor a Catholic and my name is not Mary.'

"Yes, Mary, I am a widow myself. My wife, God Rest Her Soul, was taken from me ten years ago" "So, are you a widow yourself, Mary?".

Seemed to be widows were in demand. I did strike up one literate conversation with a man named Dougie who I arranged to meet that evening for a drink. He even called me Nicci.

I arranged to meet Dougie at nine o'clock in the lobby of a local hotel. As I was parked up in my Beast just next door to this hotel, I didn't mind the lateness of the date. But, just before 7pm I received a text from Dougie to say he was on his way so could we meet earlier? There was no time to change my outfit, and decided I looked okay as I was. I hugged Milo, gave him a, *'I'm going to the shop's',* biscuit, locked the van and walked to the hotel. I got there before Dougie and took up residence on a large couch with a view of the main door. I realised I had no idea what he looked like, as I observed a whole coach load of pensioners spill into the hotel foyer. A few of them looked over at me, but none approached. I also realised Dougie had no idea what I looked like and could quite possibly be in the foyer now, chatting up random little old ladies. Then I saw him. Somehow, I knew it was him. He was wearing a big bright floral shirt which just about covered his large protruding belly, his wide smile gleamed below his large red bulbous nose. 'Jolly' I thought, as I sank into the couch when Dougie plonked himself next to me.

Our date was short. Dougie was indeed a jolly character, so jolly in-fact that every-time he said something, which he thought was funny, he would slap my leg, hard. After about ten minutes of this my leg was beginning to sting. I put up with about another ten minutes by clenching my thigh muscle whenever I heard him laugh, this numbed the slap slightly. But eventually, me being me, rather than tell him to stop slapping my leg I pretended the sulphur water I had drunk earlier in the day was not mixing well with my glass of wine. I was feeling a bit unwell and would unfortunately have to leave. Dougie was quite understanding with this lie and was more than keen to arrange another date with me, if I was staying in his area? I enthusiastically agreed to a second date. I am rubbish with the truth. Dougie was a perfectly decent man, just not the man for me.

Back at my motor-home I fumbled in the dark trying to find my keys in the bottom of my handbag. I pulled out my torch to assist me in locating them, but, I had inadvertently grabbed a hold of my rape alarm by mistake, thus setting off a high-pitched screech, right across the car-park. Milo was now jumping up at the door and barking hysterically, the van was rocking and I was cursing. Alarmingly, not a soul came to my rescue. Worrying.

The next few days involved some more fun for me. I got to go on a boat trip, organised by Pat, on the waters below the Cliffs of Moher. Donnie, who runs Doolin2AranFerries, assisted me on board whilst telling me that there are 40,000 birds on the cliffs.

"Have you counted them, Donnie?" I asked, also wondering if he counted his wives and money.

"Yes, Nicci, every hour on the hour, and there was one missing this morning!" He laughed, giving me a wink.

The boat trip was breath-taking as we bounced across the waves and Donnie was right: there certainly were thousands of birds nestling into the rugged towering cliffs.

I followed up my boat trip with a few days of exploring and ended up completely lost on the Burren, trying to find the famous 'Father Ted's' house. This proved to be a fruitless search, I found perfume houses, yoga schools, chocolate factories and an abundance of historic monuments, but no Father Ted's House. Having driven around the Burren for about two hours I parked up on a hill top trying to find my bearings, when my phone rang. The call came from Ray Darcy of RTE radio, requesting a catch-up interview. During this live interview, Ray informed me he had just that minute received a message from the Radisson Blu hotel in Galway. The Radisson Blu had very kindly offered me a complimentary hotel room, as a gift for the night of my fiftieth birthday next week. This wonderful news had me practically scream out loud. Even though the odds where I would probably be in the room alone, having not had much success finding a beau, I didn't care. Because, there would be a bath! A big, hot, bubbly bath. The thing I missed the most on this adventure. Add to that a bed - on the floor, no ladder involved, a ceiling I wouldn't bang my head on, and an evening of stillness – no rocking sensation whilst I slept. Oh yes, I felt more than happy with this news.

I eventually found my way off the Burren, having not found Father Ted's House, and discovered a lovely spot to wild camp on Traught beach. We spent two nights on this beach and bore witness to some random goings on – a man walking a goat on a lead, cows paddling in the ocean and a life size statue of Jesus in the field behind our van. Salthill, our next destination, lay across the bay.

We had been invited to stay with Ann, a lady who had written to me via my blog and invited us to stay on her small camp-site, on the beach at Salthill. Ann proved to be an absolute character and her dog, Tara, was her best friend. Like myself, she had travelled various destinations with her dog and had many a story to share. Ann's camp-site was tiny and held six static caravans affording us just enough space to park near the entrance, next to the wheelie bins. The weather had started to warm up and our van was unfortunately now homing all the flies from the wheelie bins. But I was grateful for the safe location and the lady in the static van beside us had allowed me to plug into her electric supply – having taken up my offer of five euros in payment.

That afternoon I arranged to meet another gentleman Willie Daly had matched me with. This particular gentleman had telephoned me every day for a week requesting a date. "God willing" he had said at the end of every call.

I arrived at the Salthill Hotel and took a seat on the veranda, taking in the splendid view of the busy promenade. I had arrived on time but my date was extremely late. I didn't mind, as I happily sipped my large glass of wine, watching all the people walking along the promenade. When my date eventually did arrive, my first impression was; he looked as if he had dressed for a funeral; black suit, white shirt, black tie. He appeared to be aged in his late seventies and struggled to seat himself in the chair, because, he informed me, he had just recovered from major knee surgery. He also told me of his recent operation for a neck injury, which hadn't gone so well and was now causing a lot of pain in his spine. But all this would be fine, he continued to tell me, because his spinal surgery appointment had been booked and his medication was helping.

"Nicci, you're a fine-looking woman" he said. "Are you a widow?" "I myself am a widow, ten years gone. God rest her soul" He said, with a tear in his eye.

"My wife was a fine woman, a fine woman indeed. She took good care of me." He continued.

"Nicci, if you became my wife, I promise you would have a fine life, a fine life indeed. I would only require from you to assist with my daily medication and to keep a good home. And, you would have access to my car, on a weekly basis, to visit the shops. It's a Volvo, it is."

"Gosh..." I answered, not quite knowing how to respond.

"I've been on Willie's books for some time now and unfortunately, I have not met a suitable lady." He continued.

"I specifically told Willie I would not entertain a lady who smoked, and yet my previous date was a smoker." He huffed. "Quite unacceptable."

"Oh, that is unfortunate." I replied and reached for my cigarettes from my handbag.

"I too am a smoker." I said, gleefully lighting up a cigarette.

He studied my face for a moment and then said "I could tell you were a smoker Nicci, from all the lines upon your face. But that is fine, I do not mind if you smoke."

Our date ended. I watched as he slowly hobbled across the car-park and drove off in his Volvo. I sat back down, ordered another large glass of wine and wondered if he would ever find himself a carer.

The next day, I felt a little downhearted. Not because of my disastrous date, but because the Radison Blu hotel were fully booked for the night of my fiftieth birthday. My night of luxury had to be rebooked, for the week after my birthday. So, tomorrow I would celebrate being fifty; as a single woman living next to a wheelie bin.

I cheered myself up and caught a bus into Galway city centre. Milo was not allowed on the bus.

"One return ticket to the city centre please." I told the bus driver.

"It is 2.20-euros one way or 4.60-euros return." The bus driver informed me.

"Erm, I'll have two one-way tickets then, thank you"

Galway city centre throbbed with a buzz of activity. Buskers entertained on every street corner, pavement cafés were full of hip and happy people, and pubs spilled out into the streets with Irish music blaring from each one. The sun shone brightly and all the people appeared carefree, young and trendy. Me; I felt like an old hag, sitting alone, in a bar, nursing a pint of Guinness.

"A tattoo!" I said out-loud, to the bemusement of the other customers.

Yes, I would get a tattoo. Having never been tattooed before and always having been quite against the idea, I decided to get one before I turned fifty, tomorrow. I finished my Guinness and skipped up the road in search of a parlour. There were plenty of signs advertising this service and I chose one hidden up a little side street. Having climbed the three flights of steep stairs I arrived in a dimly lit room to be greeted by a sullen looking, heavily tattooed, young girl.

"Hello, I wonder if you could tell me how much a tattoo would cost?" I asked her.

"Well, that all depends on what design you want." She answered, eyeing me up and down.

"Oh, just a dot." I answered.

"A dot?" She replied.

"Yes, just a dot, on the sole of my foot." I told her confidently.

"Prices start at fifty euros, therefore your 'dot' will cost you fifty euros." She told me defiantly.

To this day I remain untattooed. Sticking with my motto of: would you put bumper stickers on a Lamborghini?

Well I didn't enjoy that. A Fair she called it. So many people bumping into me and all those poor creatures trapped in small cages, crying. Mee kept me on my lead, which was fine by me, I was not going to leave her side today. Those poor creatures in cages were being sold to the highest bidder. And, as I'm well aware of her financial woes at the moment, I was not going to let her sell me! Not that I believe she actually would sell me, but obviously, being as handsome as I am it goes without saying someone was likely to offer her a hefty sum of money for me.

Chapter 11

Happy birthday to me. Fifty years old. Fifty and a failure. Setting myself a goal of finding the man of my dreams before I hit fifty had possibly been one of my daftest ideas. My track record quite clearly proves that I am really, rather fussy when it comes to men. Maybe fussy is too strong a word? Maybe I'm just not willing to settle for less? Less than I feel I deserve. I'm not looking for perfect, more like a man 'who just gets me'. I've never really been one for needing exceedingly good looks when it comes to a man; fool's gold is that; under the shiny exterior does not always lie a good man.

It wasn't all bad, I'd booked into a rather nice camp-site in Salthill called O'Hallorans and the lady on reception had given us a warm welcome, having recognised us from our TV appearance. I'd also arranged to meet a gentleman friend for morning coffee on the beach front. Austin originated from my home-town, and although I'd never met him, he had followed my story through my blog. He happened to be touring Ireland and was in Salthill the morning of my birthday. He arrived at the coffee shop and handed me a large bottle of champagne.

"Celebrate in style, Nicci." Austin said.

"Thank you very much. I'll save it for my hotel night, Austin, when I know I won't have to drive." I thanked him.

I hoped Austin didn't think that was an invitation? As sweet as he was, he was not the man for me.

With my champagne in hand I walked along the beach back to the campsite; casually doing an impromptu live radio interview on the way, with KCLR radio.

Back in my van I opened the two birthday cards I had carried with me since starting our trip. They both contained large amounts of money and cheered me up no end. I'd also bought myself a huge selection of chocolate and crisps and some tasty biscuits for Milo. So, here I was; fifty, still single, sitting in my van with Milo, surrounded by chocolate and wondering where to go next. Then my phone rang.

The call came from a production company called Big Mountain. The gist of the call was; they were filming a TV series starring the Irish celebrity Ardal O'Hanlon. Their TV series would be following the route of an old Victorian guidebook, written hundreds of years ago, tempting the English over to the Emerald Isle. Ardal would be filmed meeting up with various people who make this country the great nation it is. And for some reason, they wanted to meet me - a crazy, middle-aged English-woman, travelling in a van with her dog, looking for love. Apparently, the route I had travelled so far, mirrored that of the Victorian guidebook. And, the fact that I had enlisted the help of Willie Daly, they said, would make good TV. Well, why not? I thought. What have I got to lose?

My only gripe being, I had to backtrack my route to meet up with them, returning to the town of Lisdoonvarna. Although as a consolation they kindly offered to cover my travel expenses. So, two days later, off we went, back to Lisdoonvarna.

Arriving in Lisdoonvarna, I parked up in a quiet spot, in the town centre car-park and waited for them to arrive. And when they did arrive, I had a fleeting moment of feeling like a Hollywood movie star; Two large blacked out vehicles, filled with an array of technical equipment and a production crew of six. We were all introduced and I was then fitted with a microphone by a rather tall, dark and handsome, sound engineer.

"You don't mind if I put my hand down your blouse do you, Nicci?" He asked in a somewhat professional manner.

"Oh, gosh no, not at all, young man." I replied in a somewhat flirty manner. He displayed no reaction at all. He was so out of my league.

Once the crew were all set up, my instructions were to; open my van door when Ardal knocked, and invite him in.

I heard them shout action followed by a loud knock at my door. Grinning like a Cheshire Cat I opened the door and there stood Ardal.

"Nicci." He said "I believe you are looking for Willie... to help you find love..."

"You can't say that!" I squealed. And they assured me this introduction would be cut. It wasn't.

Ardal sat next to me on the couch inside my van and Milo jumped up too, choosing to sit, practically, on my lap. The cameraman just about fitted through the door and once again the director shouted "Action!". A series of questions from Ardal, all about my adventure so far, went on for about an hour. Towards the end of filming, Ardal pointed out that maybe my lack of dating success could possibly be blamed on Milo. I looked at him confused, until he pointed out that Milo had just let out a rather smelly fart! All which had been captured on film.

Due to the lack of space inside my Beast, all the questions had to be repeated once again by Ardal, but this time with the camera focused on his face. Ardal sat in the same position, asking me the same questions all the while making relevant facial expressions as if I was replying to these questions. Acting at its best and all a strange experience for me, as I sat silently, aware of the big camera behind my head.

The light-hearted interview had lasted for about an hour, although I was well aware this would probably be edited into about a ten second slot. The producer then asked if I would be willing to meet them, later that evening, in Ennistymon. They were intending to film me inside Willie Daly's pub 'Daly's Bar' being matched up with a suitable gentleman. Why not? I said.

That evening, having parked up in a side street near Dalys Bar, I applied my lipstick, brushed my hair and gave Milo his usual *'I'm going to the shop's'* biscuit. When I got to the bar, it buzzed, a real hive of activity. The location crew filled half the bar. Locals crammed the other half of the bar, jostling to take a selfie photograph with Ardal O'Hanlon. Willie spotted me through the crowd and after ordering me a pint of Guinness he ushered me to a quiet corner, where we chatted about my potential match.

"I have the perfect match for you tonight, Nicci" Willie enthused.

"You see Nicci, I picture you matched with a gentleman who has eyes of green, or maybe blue, or possibly brown. He will be a tall man or maybe your height, he is possibly of an age with you or slightly older. His hair will be dark or fair or red. He will be a good man Nicci, his nature befitting yours." Willie told me in his charming Irish accent, with a glint in his eyes. I took all this information onboard and decided Willie was possibly as confused as me, as to what I was looking for in a man.

With the camera rolling I sat down ready to be introduced to Kevin, my match. Ah, Kevin. Sweet little, four-foot-nothing, Kevin. I didn't dare stand up as we were being introduced, remembering Willie how had told me there were twenty-nine and a half men to each woman in the world: and wondering if I had just met the half? I believe the camera possibly caught my 'I don't know what to say' facial expression, as I just smiled, slightly open mouthed, at Kevin. Ardal sat opposite me, hidden behind the camera, with a wide grin on his face telling me; he knew exactly what I was thinking. The crew filmed the slightly awkward conversation between Kevin and myself and then asked me to join Ardal for a verdict. Ardal and I both agreed that Willies magic powers had not worked on this occasion. As lovely as Kevin was, he was not the man for me.

Late into the evening, the TV crew left, having handed me one hundred euros, and I was keen to get back to Milo in the van. I had earlier Googled a camp-site for tonight's stay, but now it was far too late to check-in. Willie seemed more than keen for me to stay at his house but; I declined his offer, politely made my excuses, unwrapped his arm from round my waist and headed off into the night.

Back in the van Milo seemed pretty pleased to see me, jumping from couch to couch and sniffing each new scent I'd brought back with me from the pub. Poor Milo did not like being on his own in the van at night, especially so tonight, as the heavy rain fell from the dark black sky, bouncing loudly on our tin roof. I gave Milo his good boy biscuit, started the engine and hastily drove out of Ennistymon, not knowing where on earth I was going. We kept on driving for about thirty minutes, along narrow country lanes, my headlights barely picking up the dark road in front of me and my wipers struggling with the torrential rain. On a sharp bend of one particular lane I actually saw a man, carrying a pig under his arm and squeezing through the hedge into the field beyond. I doubt anyone will ever believe this is what I saw.

Eventually we reached the town of Ballyvaughn and pulled into a large, vacant car-park opposite a church. We were the only vehicle here and I could just about make out, under the dimly lit street light, the white lines of the parking bays. I parked up the Beast, parallel with the hedges and decided this would be a good, safe place to bed down for the night.

Early the next morning, hearing a loud commotion from outside, I rubbed my eyes and peeped through a gap in my curtains. The previously empty car-park from last night was now full to the brim with hundreds of cars and hundreds of people who were all milling around, wearing what looked like running gear. It transpired that today the annual Ballyvaughn Marathon Challenge would take place and here was I parked up at the starting point. Obviously had I known this information I would have entered this marathon!

Luckily, I had no plans for the day ahead, because the Beast was now blocked in from every angle. I spent the entire day wandering around the town with Milo, had three coffee stops, visited the farmer's market and sat on a hay bale listening to the live musical performances. I even bumped into my friend, Julie from Lisdoonvarna; I felt like a local.

We don't usually have visitors in the Beast, but today was the exception. One of these visitors sat right up close to her on my couch. I didn't know who he was or what he was doing in our Beast, so I squashed myself in-between them and rested my head on Mee's lap. This man chatted to her for ages and another man stood in the doorway just watching them with a large contraption on his shoulder. There were more people outside, and I even saw one man put his hand right inside Mee's top. She stood there letting him and had this ridiculously, dopey look on her face as he did so. None of them seemed to pay me any attention whatsoever, so, I know I shouldn't have, but whilst they were talking, I let out one of my exceptionally smelly, held in farts. That got me noticed.

Chapter 12

Today I woke feeling happy. My night of luxury lay ahead, a complimentary stay at the Radisson Blu hotel in Galway city centre. If it hadn't been for my interview with RTE Radio1 I would never have received this wonderful gift for my fiftieth birthday, I felt so grateful. The only down side of my happy mood came with pangs of guilt at leaving Milo alone in the Beast overnight. Regrettably no dogs allowed.

I pulled up outside the grand entrance of the hotel and immediately noticed the looming overhead height restrictions leading into their car-park, no way was the Beast going to fit under. Then I spotted one single parking space on the road, situated right in front of the large, glass fronted, reception area of the hotel, so I parked up and headed inside. The hotel foyer projected an opulent atmosphere, the central focus being a stunning glass lift leading to all floors. I stood waiting my turn at reception, whilst observing the luxury before me; deep leather couches, low ornate tables, an abundance of beautiful fresh flowers in ceramic vases, and floor to ceiling glass windows; offering a wonderful view of my tired, old and rather scruffy looking Beast parked up at the door!

The gentleman on the desk gave me a warm and friendly welcome and assured me it would be absolutely fine to leave the Beast there overnight. He also informed me that my mother had been in touch and had booked me a treatment of my choice to be taken at their Spa. Not only that, I had also been provided with a bottle of fizz in my room, compliments of an anonymous gentleman following my adventure on Facebook. The receptionist went on to advise me that I should probably book a table for dinner in the hotel restaurant, as it did tend to get rather busy. I duly obeyed.

Clutching my room key, with instructions to take the lift up to the top floor, I quickly scuttled past all the smartly dressed guests, suddenly aware I hadn't changed out of my muddy wellies. Inside the lift, a little sign stated: only persons in possession of a fifth-floor key-card are allowed access to this floor. I began to feel a little bit special and hoped the glares from the guests below would follow my exit onto the fifth floor.

Arriving at my room I held my key against the lock and heard the smooth click of the door unlocking. Then I slowly opened the door and stepped inside. Just the act of stepping through the door provided me with a feeling of bliss; no hunting for the correct key on my van bunch, no portable steps to climb up, no hoisting myself up with the Beast's grab handle, no boisterous dog barging past me to get in first. No, I just stepped through the door and into my haven.

Wow! was an understatement. I had been booked into the penthouse. The lobby entrance was bigger than my Beast. The sumptuous, king size bed, swamped in white linen and resembling a fluffy white cloud was also bigger than my Beast. Resisting the urge to dive into my fluffy white cloud I dropped my handbag onto one of my three couches and headed outside onto my wrap around balcony. The sun belted down, beckoning me to lay on one of the inviting sun loungers. From this position I beheld the panoramic views spanning right across the harbour. Ten minutes later and sporting a rosy pink face I headed back inside my penthouse to explore some more. Suddenly remembering the best bit, I excitedly kicked off my wellies, and feeling the softness of the carpet under my feet I padded towards the bathroom. Oh, my word, a sight for sore eyes indeed; marbled from floor to ceiling, two large sinks, a massive walk in power-shower, sumptuous soft towels that had never been used to rub down a muddy Labrador and a proper real toilet that I would not have to traipse across a camp-site to empty! And then the bath. A big, deep and very inviting bath. Feeling tempted to jump in right there and then, but realising I hadn't brought my luggage up from the van yet, I decided my bath would have to wait. I went back into my bedroom and sank into on one of the couches, still absorbing the five-star feeling the room gave me. Then I spotted the bottle of fizz, in the ice bucket, with two crystal glasses placed beside it. A little pang of sadness came over me, so I poured two glasses and toasted myself, twice.

Back in the van I gathered together my belongings for the evening and sat on the couch beside Milo.

"Hey, Baby, I'm going to the shops." I lied. "It's a big shop, I might be a while, but you will be fine." His head tilted from side to side absorbing my words. God, I felt so guilty leaving him. Before I left, I placed a note on the dashboard stating that; Milo was fine, he had not been abandoned, and please contact reception if any problems.

Back in my penthouse I got straight to the most important task of the day: having my bath. I gathered together every single bottle of posh bubble bath provided and poured their entire contents under the taps, until all I could see was a mountain of foamy white bubbles. Then grabbing my glass of fizz, I eagerly stepped into the beckoning water. I slowly sank back, and disappeared under the bubbles absorbing an overwhelming feeling of relaxation and contentment throughout my whole body. This was not only my first bath in what felt like ages, it was also the first time, in a long time, that I had felt relaxed in a bathroom. To just lie back, knowing that nobody was at all likely to walk in on me, felt good. I was in a safe place. This was my bathroom, my very own bathroom, and I would own it for a whole 24 hours. Bliss, pure bliss. I didn't ever want to get out.

But, get out I did because I had a dinner reservation to get ready for and I intended to make myself look half decent whilst dining in this bustling restaurant, because you never know, there could be a handsome businessman seated at the table next to me.

Upon my arrival at the restaurant, I immediately questioned if there was another restaurant? No. This was the only restaurant, unless I would prefer to eat at the bar? The waiter told me. I scanned all the empty tables before me and wondered why I had been encouraged to reserve a table? I was the only diner.

Even though my accommodation was complimentary, I would be responsible for paying my food bill. Studying the menu carefully, looking for the cheapest item my budget could afford, I settled on a burger and a side order of chips. Presented with the drinks menu I ordered a glass of water, tap water, and wished I'd had the hindsight to bring along my left-over fizz. The staff were all extremely attentive, probably due to the fact that I was the only diner who actually needed any attention, or maybe they felt sorry for me? They had all, in turn, wished me a happy birthday.

My intention, after dinner, had been to walk into the city centre and 'hit some bars'. This plan quickly diffused upon entering my van. Having gone to check on Milo, I felt so guilty leaving him alone, I curled up next to him on the couch. I sat stroking the top of his head until eventually he fell asleep. But like a baby, every time I stood up to leave, Milo would lift his head, hand me his paw and crush me with his Labrador sad eye look. I spent my entire evening with him.

Late into the night having eventually hardened up to Milo's tricks, I returned to my penthouse. Here I fell, rather than climbed, into my bed, did a few star shapes, just because I could, and fell into a fitful sleep. The next morning, I woke very early, threw on some clothes and went straight to the van to see Milo.

After a walkabout with Milo, I returned to the hotel and headed to the breakfast buffet. Chocolate croissants, chocolate muffins and an endless supply of coffee put me in good spirits. Then I made my way to the Spa for a thoroughly enjoyable birthday massage.

Back in my penthouse, reluctantly gathering up my belongings, sad to be checking out, my phone rang. It was my dear friend, Ali. Ali is the aunt of my best friend Sue and lives on the coast of Portugal. Ali wished me a happy birthday, made some general chit chat and then threw me a massive curve ball.

"Nicci, I've been reading between the lines of your blog." she told me. "I have my suspicions that you're not very happy?"

"Oh, Ali, I'm fine." I replied.

"So where are you off to after the hotel?" Ali enquired.

"Oh, I don't know. I'll probably just keep following the coast."

"And then what, Nicci? Do you have a plan?" She pushed.

"Er, no, not really. Just take one day at a time. Enjoy the journey until my money runs out and keep my fingers crossed that I'll meet my Prince Charming." I laughed.

"Nicci, I have a proposition for you." Ali said.

"Oooh, I'm intrigued, tell me more." I enthused.

"How would you like to come and live with me, in Portugal, with Milo?"

Well that threw me. Ali lived in Foz de Arelho, a beautiful hidden gem on the Atlantic coast of Portugal. She lived in a massive beach house, with her mother - Sue's Grandmother.

Gran, who I was very fond of, had vascular dementia and required 24-hour care. Ali put her offer on the table – help her with caring for Gran in return for free, luxury accommodation in a stunning location with an endless supply of chocolate and wine thrown in for good measure.

Gran's day to day requirements were met by her twice daily nurse visits, the upkeep of the household duties were provided by Clarice, the housekeeper and the land was maintained by Andre, the gardener. My role was to be a support for Ali, to allow her some extra freedom to work, travel and also plan her daughter's forthcoming wedding to be held at the Big Beach House.

Ali also mentioned that a dear friend of hers was quite interested in utilising my services as a part-time chauffeur. He had recently had his driving licence revoked and required an occasional driver.

Ali had given me a lot to think about and told me to take a few days to mull it over. No pressure, she stated. No pressure indeed!

After reluctantly checking out of the hotel I returned to the Beast, packed away my overnight bag and roared up the engine. I could see some rather well to do guests in my wing mirror, watching me chug away, choke fumes pouring out of my exhaust, probably wondering how on earth I had afforded a night in the penthouse.

Where I was headed, I didn't know. I just felt happy to be back in my van with Milo. I decided I would just keep driving until I no longer wanted to, all the while mulling over my Portugal offer.

Mee didn't come home last night. I saw where she went, I peeped out the window and watched her enter the big glass building. I sat there for hours, never taking my eyes off the door she had entered. Eventually she came back out, gave me loads of biscuits and cuddled up on the couch with me. She looked really nice, she smelt of flowers and seemed rather overdressed to be sitting in the Beast with me. Mee sat with me for ages, every now and then she would get up off the couch and then for some reason changed her mind and sat back down again.

Eventually she got up and went back into the glass building. I was quite glad, as it was now really late and I was exhausted. She stayed in that glass building all night and came back so early in the morning that I was still asleep and was woken by the sound of her jangling keys in the door. She gave me my breakfast, walked me round the block and then once again went into that glass building. This time when Mee came back, she seemed a bit distracted by something, I didn't make too much fuss and just took up my usual position behind her seat, and off we drove.

Chapter 13

Having left Galway in a bit of a tizzy I stopped after just a few miles and pulled into a camp-site called Spiddal Mobile Home Park. The camp-site owner was very friendly and quite interested in the story of my adventure so far. I graciously refused his marriage proposal offer but I did accept his copy of The Farmers Journal, which, he told me, would provide me with a prospective husband. It didn't.

The next day, our road took us to the Lettermore peninsula, a series of islands linked together by stone-built roads. We coasted along in the Beast, driving to the very end of the islands, where the road abruptly ended, before turning around and heading back. We then came to a stop, beside a beautiful area of land, filled with large patches of Atlantic seawater. I decided this would be a great spot to spend the night. Not wishing to ever offend anyone when parking up my Beast I walked over to the only house I could see, to request permission to park overnight. Having knocked on the door, the very friendly owner said it would be fine indeed, indeed it would, for me to park up there for the night. Our camp spot provided us with a beautiful orange sunset and I even managed to capture one of those photographs where you hold the sun inside your heart shaped fingers. Milo and I both slept peacefully all night and awoke to the sound of gentle, lapping water beside the van. Milo loved his early morning swim, he did indeed, indeed he did.

We were still on the Lettermore islands and, having taken a few wrong turns, I was now approaching a dead end. I reached the end of the road with the intention of performing a three-point turn, or ten, and then re-joining the main highway. But when I stopped and saw the stunning beach in front of me, I decided to park up and explore. I must say this was possibly my favourite beach of all in Ireland. Beach Strand Tra, a sublime and tranquil paradise. Soft white sand between my toes, crystal clear water gently lapping the shore and not a soul in sight. With the sun beating down, I threw a towel onto the sand and lay back, blinking into the clear blue sky. Milo was in his element, splashing in and out of the water, exploring rock formations and digging in the sand. We stayed there all day and the only human contact I had was with a knight in shining armour. Sitting upon a throne shaped rock, staring out across the ocean, I saw, on the distant sands, a man on horseback, galloping towards me. OK, so he wasn't quite a knight in shining armour, more of an old guy just riding a horse. But he stopped when he saw me and declared, in a voice befitting a knight in shining armour "Good day to you, my fair lady. May I say, I do believe you are the most beautiful sight I have ever seen upon this beach." Being quite taken aback by his words, I didn't know how to react to this compliment and just sat bewildered and open mouthed. Then, in the blink of an eye, he departed, galloping off into the sunset, hotly pursued by his bemused and equally bewildered class of horse trekking students.

Upon leaving the Lettermore peninsula, we headed inland and stopped overnight in Cong. A charming town with a ruined medieval abbey and a castle previously owned by the Guiness family. After a long walk beside the river Cong we wandered back towards the town. Here in the town centre stood a bronze statue, depicting the characters of John Wayne and Maureen O'Hara from the 1951 film 'The Quiet Man'. I, quite innocently, hooked Milo's lead onto the hand of Maureen, and Milo stood there, quite patiently, whilst I took a photograph, only to then be surrounded by a group of tourists wanting to take a photo of John Wayne, Maureen O'Hara and their pet dog!

After one night, at a fairly expensive, but pleasant camp-site in Cong, we drove to Westport where I had prearranged to meet up with a couple I knew from my home-town. That evening, we all sat in their local on the quay, The Helm, and enjoyed a delicious meal of crab lollipops. During this meal I received a telephone call from Ali in Portugal.

"Nicci, I need Milo's measurements." she said. "Nose to tail length, height, weight, everything."

"For?" I asked.

"I've found a cheap flight from Manchester to Lisbon, for you and Milo, next week."

This was Ali all over. If you didn't make a decision, she would make it for you. Ali had 'live life to the full' running through her veins. I was going to Portugal.

I bid an early farewell to my friends and headed back to the van. Here I found a metal tape measure and went about trying to measure Milo as accurately as I could. I then Googled how I would get back to the UK in time to catch my flight over to Lisbon. This involved driving across country from Westport to Dublin, to pick up a ferry crossing over to Liverpool and also fit in a vet check 24 hours before the ferry departure, to allow Milo re-entry into the UK. In the midst of this turmoil my head was spinning. But I was also rather excited.

We left the west coast of Ireland and began our lengthy drive across to the east coast, towards Dublin. We stopped off for two nights en-route, one at a peaceful and rural location beside a canal and one in an absolute hellish camp-site which was far too crowded and way overpriced. Plus, being a sunny weekend, this seemed to convince all the men in the camp-site to wear wife beater vests and baseball caps, whilst swigging beer from tins.

Arriving in Dublin, having taken Milo for his early morning vet check in the city centre, I parked up the Beast on the Dollymount Strand, just a stone's throw away from the ferry terminal. This being our last night in

Ireland before our ferry back to the UK in the morning. After a long walk on the beach with Milo, we both settled down for sleep. I couldn't sleep. I lay awake for hours just thinking about my past, my present and my future.

What had I done? What was I doing? And what was I going to do?

Last year I'd made a brave (or was it crazy?) decision to leave behind the life I once had, and I definitely had no regrets about that. My whole life had been what I perceived it to be and I was mainly happy with it so far. I do believe you can look back and view your life however you want to; glass half empty or glass half full, you and only you control that perception. Looking to the future is, I believe, also down to you. People will achieve what they choose to achieve. We all set our own goals, governed by our own capabilities. In my head: my future looked bright. So, therefore, I decided, I owned my past and I owned my future. But the present was the bit that flummoxed me. The present was the here and the now. The moment I was in and the moment I was experiencing: but somehow struggled to feel a part of. Therefore, had I ever done what I really and truly wanted to do? And was I really and truly going to dictate my own future? No wonder I couldn't sleep that night!

There were no problems boarding the Beast onto the ferry back to Liverpool. The crossing was calm and even Milo seemed quite relaxed.

I stood on deck of the ship, leaving the Port of Dublin, watching the land slowly disappear on the horizon. I'd certainly enjoyed Ireland; the people, the scenery and the craic. I hadn't achieved what I'd set out to on the love front, but I'd had a jolly good time trying. No regrets, none at all.

Here we go again 'We're going on an adventure, Milo' she tells me. What next, I wonder? Apparently, she's been thrown a curve ball. Well I never

73

saw it, if I'd seen it, I would have surely caught it. She tells me an opportunity has presented itself and we are flying to a place called Portugal. I'm sure she said 'fly'. Don't know what that's all about, I can't fly and I'm damn sure Mee can't either. The Beast can possibly fly, but she tells me we are not taking the Beast with us. That seems strange: us going on an adventure without the Beast. Anyway, she sold it to me with the promise of a beach. And not just any beach she told me, this beach will be on our doorstep every day.

Milo and Me in Lisdoonvarna

Milo and Me on Lettermore island

Chapter 14

Our journey to Portugal was extremely stressful for both Milo and Me. In less than twelve months, having reduced my life from a three-bedroomed house into a motor-home, I now struggled to fit it all into one suitcase. Well, in fact I actually had; two large suitcases, one large holdall and a rather bulky handbag. Added to that Milo plus his huge travel crate, and we only just about fitted into my mum's car for our drive to Manchester airport.

On arriving at the airport, we made our way to the cargo area to organise Milo's transportation onto the aircraft. There seemed to be much confusion here and eventually after much toing and froing between departments, the airline staff at the cargo centre informed me; Milo was booked in as excess baggage and was to check in, with me, in the terminal building at the customer check-in desk.

"The building which says 'No dogs allowed'?" I questioned.

"Yes, Madam, you and Milo must join the queue at the TAP Airline check-in desk and present your tickets." the gentleman duly informed me.

Mum stayed in the car and Pip helped us through the main departure's hall. Pip pushed one trolley holding Milo's huge crate, I pushed another trolley piled high with both my suitcases, my holdall, my handbag and Milo, nervously, walking on his lead by my side. We did get some funny looks upon joining the queue at check-in. I think most people thought Milo was my guide dog.

At the desk I presented our tickets and passports. Milo sat, obediently, at my feet, observing all, whilst the lady checked our documents. Then she placed my suitcases on the luggage belt and directed us to the excess baggage desk to check Milo in. Here, they weighed and scanned Milo and instructed him to enter his crate. Milo looked up at me with his big sad eyes, ears low and his body shaking. He didn't know what was going on, but he sensed it wasn't going to be pleasant. Milo reluctantly entered the crate, where I had placed his favourite blanket and a t-shirt smelling of me. The inside walls of the crate also held my scent, as I had previously spent some time inside it, trying to encourage Milo to believe this was a safe place; no mean feat squeezing myself into that crate. Once inside the crate Milo just sat there, staring at me through the mesh, whimpering quietly, oblivious to his journey ahead. He looked so frightened and I felt his fear.

"I love you, Baby. You be a good boy. Everything's okay and I'm just going to the shops." I lied through my tears. And off he went, through a wide swing door, with the baggage handlers.

"I love you Milo." I shouted out as he disappeared.

"Oh, Pip." I cried. "He looks so scared."

"He'll be fine, Nicci," she reassured me. "As will you."

"And remember," she continued "If you're not happy in Portugal you just come straight home to me, I'm always going to be here for you. And of course, Milo. And don't worry about your Beast, I will take good care of him while you're away." Pip added.

Pip and I hugged. Then off she went, as I quickly headed up to the departure lounge. I found myself a seat near to the big window at the boarding gate. And then I saw Milo. Well I saw his crate, perilously placed on a baggage trolley under the aircraft wing. I stood at the window with my hands and face pressed against the glass, watching the baggage handlers chuck the suitcases into the hold. Milo was the last to be put into the hold. I willed those men to be kind to him, to be gentle lifting his crate and to utter him a few words of comfort as they placed him into this dark, unfamiliar and noisy place. Surely, Milo must be wondering where I am?

I peeled my face from the window, wiped away my tears and sat back in my seat, oblivious to the stares from other passengers, no doubt thinking I was either a very nervous passenger or an overly sensitive yet avid plane spotter.

On-board the aircraft I was absently aware of the safety demonstration before me. Normally, being an ex-air-hostess, I always pay full attention to these demonstrations, I know how important they are. But as they got to the bit about life jackets my mind drifted off to Milo. What if we do have to ditch in the ocean? How will I save Milo? He will be trapped, under water, unable to escape his cage. My mind went into overdrive and I imagine I probably once again looked like a very nervous passenger.

The flight was long and I was fretful throughout. Eventually we arrived in Lisbon and I pretty much ran all the way to the luggage area. My suitcases eventually arrived on the belt, I piled them onto a trolley and then hurriedly went in search of Milo. I found a member of staff who directed me to an office with a long queue of people outside. I so wanted to jump to the front of the queue and shout 'sod your bicycles and your oversized suitcases! I need to save Milo.' But I didn't. I patiently waited my turn and eventually got to the front, where I was subsequently told to go back to the luggage hall where I would find Milo. I ran all the way back like a mad woman and arrived to find the luggage hall completely empty. But for a cleaner, sweeping the floor.

"My dog!" I shouted, throwing my hands up into the air. "Where is my dog?"

The poor cleaner man stared at me blankly. He spoke no English and just saw a hysterical woman screaming unknown words at him. And then, I saw, behind him, a door open and Milo's crate being pushed through on a trolley.

"Milo!" I screamed, as I barged past, nearly knocking over the poor innocent cleaner. I poked my fingers through the mesh desperately trying to stroke Milo. His crate door was bound shut with plastic ties which I was tempted to bite through with my teeth at this point. With Milo barking and my phone ringing I now had the task of trying to manoeuvre two very heavy trolleys, through the hordes of people blocking my way, to reach Ali in the arrival's hall. Fortunately, a very nice airline pilot saw my struggle and kindly offered to push one of the trolleys for me. If I hadn't been so distressed, I might have flirted with him; but my priorities lay with getting Milo out of his crate.

And there stood Ali, screaming out my name, waving frantically and now running towards us. And, she was hotly pursued by her notably handsome friend, the one whom I would be chauffeuring for. Hmm, I thought to myself, what a hunk he is. I may well be here to drive for you, but you could quite easily drive me to distraction. Mr Hunky, as I would now call him, practically snatched the trolley from the grip of the handsome airline pilot and then grabbed me in his arms like a long-lost lover.

"Nicci." he whispered into my ear, in his deep and sexy Portuguese accent. "At last you are here." I noticed handsome airline pilot averting his eyes just as Mr Hunky gave my buttocks a gentle squeeze.

The drive to Ali's house took about an hour. Far from Milo being pleased to see me, he hated me. He sat as far away from me as possible on the back seat with his face pressed against the car window. Every-time I tried to hug him he edged a little further away. I'll never know what he experienced on that aircraft, but he quite clearly blamed me.

Eventually, having dropped off Mr Hunky, we arrived at the Big Beach House in Foz do Arelho. Darkness had fallen as the big electric gates slowly opened before us. Milo must have sensed we had arrived as he seemed quite excited to be getting out of the car. That is until Ali's dog, Max, came bounding towards us and grabbed Milos neck into his clenched teeth. Milo immediately jumped back into the car and only came out when we had calmed Max down. Max was a one year old Staffy pup and his idea of play was to hang off any bigger dogs' neck. Unfortunately, Milo would have to get used to this.

Inside the house, I received a warm and welcoming hug from Clarice, the housekeeper. She had lovingly prepared us a big dish of Bacalhau, a traditional Portuguese meal of dried salty fish served with potatoes. Unfortunately, I would have to get used to this.

Whoa! I don't know quite what happened there but I think I've just been to hell. It was all going so well this morning; we all piled into the car and I thought we were going for a walk. But once outside the car, Mee put me on my lead and took me into a very busy building, full of people. I stayed close by her side, that is, until she persuaded me to enter that large box which has been lurking in the garden for the last few days. Then my day just went from bad to worse. Mee was hugging me and crying and then she disappeared out of sight through a door. I was carried outside and then placed onto some kind of lifting mechanism. There were two, quite friendly, men with me and they were chatting away to me. But then they lifted my box, said goodbye and shut the door. It took a while for my eyes to adjust in the dim light but it appeared, I was alone. I barked as loud as I could for Mee, but she didn't come. Then there was an almighty loud noise and my belly flipped inside of me. The noise never stopped, it went on for an awful long time. I kept barking but I couldn't compete with this noise around me. Eventually it did stop, just after I was jerked, quite violently against the side of my box. And then the door opened, and I could see daylight, and there were two different men talking words to me, of which I could not understand. And then I saw Mee. She was all excited and making a fuss of me. Huh! It will take a long while before I forgive her for leaving me in that box, a very long while.

Chapter 15

I woke rather early on my first day in Portugal. As I adjusted my eyes to the sight of Milo lying practically on top of me, in my bed, I realised his steely glare only confirmed I was still unforgiven.

Looking up to the ceiling, I admired the effort Ali had gone to in decorating my room, prior to my arrival. Swathes of brightly coloured fabric covered the entire ceiling, all meeting in a central point where they wrapped themselves around a large brightly patterned light shade. In the corner of the room stood a tall floor lamp, boasting three bright green arms, each stretching out towards me. Scatter cushions displaying all the colours of a rainbow lay dotted about the room. As Milo continued to stare at me, his red fur clashing slightly with my bright pink bedspread, I closed my eyes, momentarily blocking out my multi-coloured room, and thought; next time Ali asks me, what my favourite colour is? I shouldn't answer 'Oh, I don't mind, I like them all'.

Climbing out of bed I decided a walk down to the lagoon might put me back into Milo's good books. Once we had bypassed Max, Milo practically dragged me down the steep winding road towards the lagoon. I'm sure he thought I was taking him back home. As soon as we reached the sand, I let him off his lead and in true Milo spirit he bounded into the water and swam like a fish. He was so happy, bouncing in and out of the water and digging in the sand. The hot morning sun had already warmed the sand beneath my feet and there wasn't a soul in sight. That is until we walked on a little further and saw all the fishermen out in the shallow waters. Each fisherman had placed their catch of the morning safely into bags all along the shoreline, which was exactly where Milo was headed. I tried my best to catch up with him but I was too slow, Milo already had his head deep into a bag of fresh, tasty fish and was happily munching away. My rescue mission was hindered by the invisible (to my eyes) fishing lines dotted along the shore. I think I pulled down at least three lines before I finally reached Milo, yanked his collar, and dragged him up the sand bank, whilst shouting out sorry to all the angry looking fishermen. I knew, there and then, I would need to find out the Portuguese word for sorry, as, I would no doubt be using it often.

Back at the Big Beach house, Ali took me through to Gran's room to teach me how to administer her feed with feeding tubes. Vascular Dementia is a cruel and merciless affliction. It takes no prisoners. The last time I had seen Gran, the early stages of dementia had just begun to set in. She had been entertaining and yet lost. Now she was just lost. But Gran was surrounded by love: everyone loved Gran. She would never want for love, her network of support here was unlimited. And I had arrived to add to that. Gran's eyes followed me round the room as I approached her bed, I like to believe she looked pleased to see me; sadly, Gran's face has no smile, just as Gran's face has no frown. Gran's eyes tell her tale.

Once we had settled Gran into her comfy armchair beside the garden door, Ali insisted we test out her new trampoline, recently erected for the forthcoming paying guests. This started off as all good fun, until Ali wet her knickers and I nearly knocked myself unconscious. As I wobbled back to the house, I kicked Milos ball into the swimming pool and he immediately jumped in to retrieve it. This was all well and good with Milo being such a strong swimmer, but he soon discovered jumping in was easy, getting out was near impossible. I had to jump in and heave him out over the side. He never went in the pool again.

Later in the evening Ali Ggoogled Gin cocktail recipes, choosing one made with strawberries and peppercorns. Sitting outside on beanbags I told Ali all about my adventure in Ireland and she told me about all her plans for the summer ahead and the forthcoming wedding. I loved listening to Ali's stories, all spoken with her native Scottish accent. Even when she spoke in Portuguese her Scottish accent could still be heard. I believed Ali spoke perfectly fluent Portuguese, although her son told me she often made words up if she couldn't translate them; nobody ever corrected her. We chatted on into the small hours and both slept well that night.

The next few days were a mixture of work and play. Ali was in full swing preparing the upstairs of the house for paying guests, or PG's as she liked to call them. Since Ali's children had grown up and, practically, left home and her adorable husband Ze had sadly died, Ali had now moved downstairs into the basement of the Big Beach house. In saying that, the basement area consisted of a kitchen living area about the size of a football pitch, four bedrooms, four bathrooms and numerous other little rooms. Thus, giving an idea of how the other two floors above could easily accommodate numerous house guests. The mature gardens, with pine trees and palm trees, wrapped around the whole house offering complete seclusion, yet not obstructing the wonderful views of the lagoon stretching out to the Atlantic Ocean. Every night as I lay my head on my pillow, I could hear in the distance, the waves of the Atlantic crashing down dancing on the shore, that is, when Milo wasn't snoring in my ear.

My days at the Big Beach house now consisted of; waking early, feeding Milo, brewing coffee and then administering Gran's first feed. After which, I would sit with Gran telling her stories, until Clarice arrived. I always knew when Clarice had arrived at the electric gates because Milo would bark relentlessly, wag his tail and run to the door in anticipation. Clarice is what is known as a feeder. She decided, early on, that Milo was far too skinny and needed feeding up. I tried my best to convince her that Milo was in fact very healthy and lean, for a Labrador, but she was having none of it. Every single morning, she brought with her six fresh bread rolls and fed the left overs, heavily buttered, to Max and Milo. Milo adored Clarice. His constant drool confirmed this fact.

Once the nurses had washed and dressed Gran each day, I could do pretty much what I wanted. I had a timer set on my phone to remind me of all of Gran's six feeds per day - as she was never going to tell me she was hungry, bless her. If Clarice happened to be on duty in the house, Ali and I could have play days. These mainly consisted of trips to the market, lunch dates, dog walking or just exploring. Ali had an absolute knack of turning the most mundane situation into an adventure. On one particular dog walk she found the road blocked with a huge and imposing wooden barrier. She got out of the car, ignoring the 'no trespassers' sign, lifted the barrier, took the dogs out of the car and then drove off; with Milo and Max frantically running beside us down the track. Good exercise for them she declared. And the reward of a fun filled swim for them at the end of the track.

Ali insisted I drive her car on day one. I had to get used to this driving if I was to be Mr Hunky's chauffeur. I did quite well, I didn't end up in any ditches and neither did the oncoming traffic. Although Milo seemed a little confused; he had always sat behind me when I was driving the Beast, but now I was driving seated on the left side of the car and he didn't quite know where to sit.

After being in the Big Beach house for about a week, Mr Hunky arrived with my car. I had been quite excited about this because with Mr Hunky being such a well-respected character here in Foz do Arelho, I imagined my car would be a rather fast, sleek, and expensive vehicle to match. Visions of me dressed up in a smart stroke sexy uniform driving Mr Hunky to various very important business meetings came to mind. How wrong was I. My car was a Smart Car. The tiniest little car I had ever seen. After driving the Beast, I now decided this car would be named the

Mouse. Milo only just fitted his large frame onto the back shelf of the Mouse and had to duck his head every time I shut the boot. As for important business meetings; Mr Hunky only ever required me to drive him on social expeditions, more often than not involving copious amounts of alcohol on his part; possibly how he lost his licence in the first place? But Mr Hunky was a breath of fresh air and provided much entertainment during my stay in Foz.

I think I might forgive Mee for my awful experience in hell. She has certainly made up for it recently. We get to walk on the beach every day and people quite kindly leave bags of fresh fish for me on the shore line. Mee does get quite hysterical when I accept these kind offerings and has taken to shouting out "desculpa!" to all and sundry. And then there is Clarice, dear Clarice. She always has food for me. She pats my head saying "cao magro" and looks so sad. Its okay here in Portugal, a little warm for my liking but the tiled floors provide a good place to cool down. When we first arrived here, I made the schoolboy error of jumping into the swimming pool. It's very deep and has no sloping edges for me to climb out on, I certainly won't be going in there again, no matter how hot I feel. I do love Ali, she lets me lie on the couch whenever I want and she makes Mee laugh, a lot. I just need to get to grips with this Max character, he is so annoying and childish. He thinks it's fun to constantly grab my neck with his massive teeth and hang on until I bark. He needs to learn 'it's not big and it's not clever'.

Chapter 16

My first driving job for Mr Hunky came very late one evening. With the annual fiesta taking place in Nadadouro Mr Hunky asked me to drive him there and back and join him in the celebrations. The streets were bumper to bumper with cars when we arrived but this did not hinder parking the Mouse; being so small it could fit into the tiniest of parking spots. The little town of Nadadouro heaved at the edges with people, the music blaring from the centre stage and the atmosphere electric. Festa was in full swing and Mr Hunky seemed to know everyone here, stopping and speaking to his many friends I struggled to keep up with him among the crowds. Every time somebody bought Mr Hunky a drink, he insisted they bought me one too. I didn't wish to offend anyone, but obviously as I was driving, late at night and in a foreign country, I discreetly just kept pouring them onto the ground. Eventually, very late into the night, Mr Hunky suggested we depart the Festa. He was a little worse for wear and acted in high spirits during our drive back. I had no idea how to get back and his directions were basically non-existent. He also thought it would be really funny to place his hands over both my eyes just as we were approaching a sharp bend going downhill. Mr Hunky laughed out loud, as I swerved and zigzagged the Mouse desperately trying to regain control, luckily without any oncoming traffic. We eventually arrived back at his apartment: alive. I parked up at his door, engaged the handbrake and politely asked; when would he require my services again? Suddenly, out of the blue, Mr Hunky lurched forward and kissed me, passionately, on the lips. With this encounter taking me completely by surprise my immediate reaction was to pull away. It's not that I wasn't attracted to Mr Hunky, trust me he is extremely handsome and sexy to boot. But, flashing through my head were numerous reasons why this was not a good idea. The main one being that Mr Hunky, and his large family, were truly dear friends of Ali's and had been for many years. If this all went horribly wrong, and with my track record it probably would, then life would potentially become pretty awkward for me, if I wanted to stay in Portugal. So, as Mr Hunky sat there staring at me with a look of confused rejection in his big, brown, sexy eyes, I sadly told him this was not acceptable behaviour. I would be his chauffeur and his friend, but no more than that. "OK, Nicci." He casually said, in his sexy Portuguese accent. With a feeling that Mr Hunky seldom encountered rejection I sat watching, as he jumped out of the car and casually strolled toward his apartment, where at the door he turned, smiled and blew me a kiss. Damn! I thought. Damn!

Back at the Big Beach house I crawled into my bed, squeezing in next to Milo, and poured my heart out to him.

"Oh, Milo, he is so handsome." I told him.

"Everybody loves Mr Hunky, why can't I?" I bemoaned.

Milo nodded his head as if understanding, wriggled in a little closer and then fell asleep with his head resting on my leg.

The next day, Ali decided a trip to Nazare market was in order and that it would be a good idea to take Milo too. I wasn't too sure about this but went along with it.

The market bustled with shoppers as I tried to weave between the stalls, Milo pulling on his lead all the while. Milo had the constant scent of food, it was everywhere and he tried desperately to pull me towards it. Health and Safety is non-existent in these markets, loose ropes lay strewn on the ground once tied around the metal rods protruding from the stalls and supposedly supporting the tarpaulins above. Large pot holes caught me with every step. Milo, in his manic hunger, had spotted what looked like a half-eaten hamburger, unfortunately tucked way under a stall, and slightly out of reach. But this was not going to stop Milo. He dived straight in head first, under the table and with me in tow. I caught my foot in some loose rope and landed slap bang on the top of the table which was luckily stacked with piles of clothing; a soft landing on my part. With one hand still holding onto Milo's lead under the table, I used my free hand to casually pretend I was trying to reach an item of clothing towards the back of the table. The stall holder stared at me suspiciously as I lay on the table, my feet off the ground and gripping a pair of men's boxer shorts in my hand, all the while wriggling my other hand under the table trying, desperately, to pull Milo out. Eventually, Milo, having finished off the hamburger, came out from under the table and graciously pulled me off the stack of men's underwear. The stall holder was still glaring at me as I ran away, throwing back to him the boxer shorts and shouting out a friendly 'obrigada'. Ali, having witnessed this whole shenanigan, suggested we head back home and maybe not take Milo on our next market trip.

Every morning, down at the lagoon, I felt blessed to be living here. I would sit on the sandbanks, absorbing the complete tranquility the still waters of the lagoon offered, whilst throwing a ball into the water for Milo. Some days we would head down to the main beach, where in comparison to the lagoon the gigantic waves crashed like avalanches and exploded onto the shore. Milo would never go near the shore, even if his ball landed near, he would step back and expect me to retrieve it; Milo sensed the danger. But the surfers loved this danger. They were there every day, riding the waves and providing an exhilarating source of entertainment for me.

Usually, after our long walks, Milo would quite happily chill on the cool, tiled floor in the kitchen, where he had a perfect view point to watch Clarice cooking. I don't know what Clarice kept in her apron pockets but

I often caught her, out the corner of my eye, fishing things out to pop into Milo's constantly drooling mouth.

As I lay on the big couch, a part of me watching Breaking Bad and a part of me frantically trying to think up an excuse of how to decline the Bacalhau I could smell wafting over from the kitchen, Ali bounced into the room.

"I think we should introduce Milo to the 'other' dogs." She declared.

The 'other' dogs were kept in the field at the far end of the garden. Two Portuguese Mountain dogs, both the size of a small horse. These dogs weren't house pets, more of guard dog living free on the land, separated from the house by secure fences. They had picked up Milo's scent on his arrival and had both been quite restless ever since. So, Ali decided, if they met Milo, they would surely settle down thereafter.

Ali assured me this would be fine, they would just have a good old sniff of Milo and then return to their field. She then informed me she would have the hose pipe at the ready in the event of any trouble, as Portuguese Mountain dogs have a fear of water. Apparently, the sheer weight of their fur makes it impossible for them to swim so therefore they never go near water. I'm not sure if this information reassured me or terrified me.

I recalled a time, from many years ago when I had first visited Ali at the Big Beach house. I had risen very early one morning and was sitting on a wall in the garden, drinking my coffee and admiring the rising sun, when Rocky casually walked up to me. Rocky, a Portuguese Mountain dog, who has since died, stood beside me for a moment, sniffing at my bare toes. I barely took any notice of him, being far too engrossed watching the glorious sun rising through the tall pine trees. Ze, Ali's husband, watched from the gate, unable to utter a sound and held his breath whilst Rocky sniffed away. Unbeknown to me, Rocky was a highly dangerous guard dog and had very little human contact; he was only let out at night to roam the grounds and was tied up in the field during the day, for our own safety. After Rocky had finished his sniff of my feet he walked away, as casually as he had arrived. Ze breathed out and immediately took Rocky back to the field and tied him up. Ze later told me that due to my complete ignorance Rocky had smelled no fear from me and this was possibly the only reason he had chosen not to attack me. Ze went on to show me the deep scars on his own hands; all inflicted by Rocky.

Milo quite happily trotted beside me towards the gate which led into the field where the other dogs lay under a shaded tree in the distance. Ali unlocked the gate and beckoned them over. Milo suddenly stopped in his tracks as they approached, and desperately tried to squeeze himself between my legs. I felt his fear. Then everything happened so quickly; The more dominant of the two dogs came charging towards us, snarling and baring her teeth. Milo turned and shot off like a bullet towards the house. The attacking dog was now in hot pursuit of Milo as I screamed at Ali to turn on the hose. They were out of sight when I heard an almighty scream come from Milo, a long high-pitched constant scream, which sounded like a pig screeching in a slaughter house. I ran as fast as I could towards them and came upon the sight of Milo pinned to the ground with the whole of his throat inside the jaws of the attacking dog. Milo's eyes were bulging in terror, his body quivering under her grip. I could hear Ali shouting "the tap won't turn on!" as my instinct told me to save Milo. So, without thinking I grabbed at the fur on the back of the killer dog and tried desperately to pull her off Milo. Probably not my best move because she could have chosen to turn her attack onto me at any point. Fortunately, Ali suddenly appeared and shooting water all over us the killer dog loosened her grip, giving Milo the opportunity to run.

As Ali hosed the dogs back towards the field and closed the gate, she declared maybe that wasn't such a good idea, but on a good note killer dog could and would have killed Milo if she had wanted to, so therefore; she didn't want to. This did not make me feel any better as I lay on my bed trying to console poor Milo. He shook for most of the day but fortunately did not have a single wound upon him. Milo and me never went near that field again, after that traumatic day.

Oh my God! I just met one crazy bitch today. I was standing with Mee, just minding my own business having a little sniff around, when she came charging out of the big field towards me, she had this mad, crazy look in her eyes. I ran, I ran as fast as my legs would carry me but it was no good, she cornered me near the garage at the back of the house and pinned me to the ground. I was in seriously big trouble here, I thought, as I felt her massive teeth clamping around my throat. I didn't fight back, I couldn't, but I did try croaking out that "desculpa" word I hear Mee say so often. This seemed to loosen her grip slightly, but I was so worried because Mee was standing behind her and I was terrified this senseless attacker would turn on her. But then, all of a sudden, Ali appeared and showered us all with water and the crazy bitch let go of my neck. I bolted into the house, sopping wet and completely traumatised. Mee spent the rest of the day lying on the bed with me, trying to console me. I certainly do not want to meet her again, she makes Max's neck grabbing antics feel like a game of tickle.

Chapter 17

The days were slowly drifting by here in Foz do Arelho for Milo and Me. Life ticked along fairly stress free; as long as Milo avoided the field. The PG's came and went upstairs, providing a recurring routine of bed changing and laundry chores for Clarice. Clarice loved to iron, she ironed everything, often including my underwear, somehow, she managed to make all my laundry look as if it had just come straight off a shop shelf. When PG's were in the Big Beach house, we all tried to stay out of sight. As they had paid for the privilege of their stay it was only fair that they should have the run of the house and grounds. It was like upstairs-downstairs; Ali and I like the hidden unseen staff, holed up in the basement, and usually hooked on our latest Netflix series. Milo and Max were no doubt frustrated by this, only being allowed to play in the garden during the early hours of the morning, but they were more than compensated with regular trips to the beach.

One day, I was waiting for a lock-smith to arrive because a PG had complained his key was sticking in the bedroom door lock. When the lock-smith arrived, I took him upstairs and using the master key, I managed to unlock the bedroom door and he followed me in. Unfortunately, the guest, who I thought had gone out for the day, was in fact just stepping out of his shower, dripping wet, looking rather shocked and very naked. I apologised profusely, turned on my heels and barged out past the equally shocked looking lock-smith. I did make a mental note though, that if a tall, dark, single, handsome PG should ever book into the Big Beach house; I could use this 'lock-smith' excuse as the perfect introduction.

I had now become a little braver exploring the local area. On Clarice days, and when Ali had gone away on business trips, I would go off on my own in the Mouse. Using my trusted sat-nav, I would drive for miles, usually stopping in coffee shops where I would exercise my favourite past-time of people watching. Today, I had decided to take Milo along with me. We had had a good old splash about on the beach and were now chilling in a beach front café. I sat quite relaxed in my white, plastic chair, just watching the world go by. That is until Milo spotted something of interest and chose to suddenly shoot off in its direction. Unfortunately, his lead was wrapped tightly around my wrist and in my relaxed and laid-back state I shot off, with him, across the ground, with the white plastic chair still attached to my sweaty backside. The bemused café owner came to my rescue and gallantly removed the chair from my backside. Once I had composed myself, I paid the bill, left an appropriate tip and decided not to take Milo on any more of my café jaunts.

Over time I had done a fair amount of chauffeuring for Mr Hunky, mainly consisting of social occasions, airport trips and the like. Mr Hunky had never tried to kiss me again and I believe we had built up a mutual respect for each other. Late one evening, as I sat watching another Netflix series, Mr Hunky telephoned requesting my services. He required just a local run to a town where he needed to pick something up. I threw on my flip flops and jumped into the Mouse. I picked up Mr Hunky outside his apartment and off we drove. We seemed to be driving for miles, it was dark and the sea mist was descending on the coast road.

"Just pull into this petrol station, Nicci." Mr Hunky instructed. "Park over there and turn off the headlights."

"Are we not getting petrol?" I asked curiously.

"No, Nicci, we wait here. For my friend." Said Mr Hunky.

"Oh, are we taking him somewhere?" I asked, wondering where he would sit, what with the Mouse only having two seats.

"No, Nicci, my friend, he does supply for me." "He will arrive soon." Said Mr Hunky, as he removed a rather large wad of euros from his back pocket.

I sat there, quite mystified, watching the petrol station close down. All the forecourt lights were turned off and the staff had locked up and left the premises. It was now just me and Mr Hunky sitting in the Mouse in a deserted, dimly lit, petrol station, waiting for his friend. Mr Hunky busily retuned the radio station, as I sat in the driver seat with my window wound down staring into the dark, misty distance. Then suddenly, out of nowhere a motorbike roared up beside me and a small package was thrown through the window and landed in my lap. I sat there for a moment wondering what on earth had just happened and then realised Mr Hunky was now out of the car and huddled up close with the helmet-clad motorbike rider. This was the exact moment I realised, with full clarity, that I was on a 'drug run' and I was sitting alone in the Mouse holding the 'goods'. My already over active imagination went into overdrive; OK, this is fine. Mr Hunky can do as he pleases, he is a grown man. But. What if this is a set up? What if his 'friend' is an undercover cop? What if Miami Vice jump out the shadows with guns blaring, and drag me out of the Mouse, throw me onto the bonnet and cuff me? What if I have to spend the next twenty years locked up in a Thai prison, every day protesting my innocence? Or worse. What if his 'friend' is a baddy drug dealer and just shoots us both dead? My ignorance in the drug dealing world had hit overdrive. Sweating profusely, my life flashed before me. Then Mr Hunky jumped back into the passenger seat, took the package from my shaking hands and said "OK, Nicci, let's go home." And off we drove, back along the misty coast road, me constantly checking my rear-view mirror, convinced we were being followed.

Back at the Big Beach house Ali was still up.

"You're back early, Sweety." Said Ali.

"Yes. But at least I am alive." I answered earnestly. And went to bed.

I saw a cat today. This is the first cat I've seen since we arrived in Portugal. Now, as anyone who knows me understands; I have to chase cats, I don't know why I do, I just do. I've never caught one, they're always too fast, and if I did ever catch one, I don't know what I would say to it. But this one was so skinny looking I reckon I could have caught it quite easily, if Mee hadn't interfered. My initial leap forward felt quite powerful but then all of a sudden, I was yanked back and I landed sprawled on the floor next to Mee; who for some reason had a chair attached to her backside. She didn't look too happy and was muttering something about never taking me to this café again. Good! I thought, as I saw that scrawny, little, Portuguese cat glaring at me from the bushes.

Chapter 18

In the morning, I told Gran all about my 'drug run' with Mr Hunky. She watched me intently, as I told her every little detail. Gran held all my secrets; I have no idea how or if she translated this information, but I knew for a fact that she would never tell a soul.

Late that morning I was lying in the hammock, under the big palm trees in the garden, the PG's having gone out for the day, when my phone rang. My phone rarely rang, unlike Ali's, which rang constantly. I looked at the screen and could see it was Mr P calling. The same Mr P who had, very nearly, provided me with my happy ever after, during our Scotland adventure. Mr P and I had remained friends and stayed in touch after the end of our romance, through the occasional phone call here and there. Answering the call, Mr P said hello and enquired as to how life was treating Milo and me in Portugal? We made some small talk and then he went on to tell me he was contemplating booking a holiday; Was I near an airport? Was the weather good this time of year? Was there much to see and do where I was?

Oh dear, I thought, is Mr P hinting at rekindling our romance? This was all the more intriguing as I had only just, the day before, received a random message on social media from a lady I had never met. Out of the blue this lady had written to tell me of how she understood all the ins and outs of my past relationship with Mr P, as apparently, she had loved him for over ten years. And still did. She told me she had been in a relationship with Mr P, that is, until she had seen us both, live on national TV one morning last year, declaring 'our' relationship to Philip and Holly. What a dreadful way to find out you're being cheated on, I thought to myself.

This lady went on to tell me; Mr P was now back in her life and he was suggesting they should go on a holiday together. She was, for some reason, seeking my advice as to what she should do? Should she go on a holiday with him? Was it definitely over with me and him? And could she trust him? she asked me. I wrote back to her saying, I don't know you, but as we probably both well knew, Mr P was a complicated character, and only she could know how to move forward with him. Ending my reply with a good luck.

And now, here was Mr P, contemplating a holiday in my neck of the woods, not at any point mentioning who he might bring with him. How funny, I thought, as I spent the next ten minutes trying to suggest various alternative destinations in the world that Mr P, and whoever, could holiday at.

Having ended our telephone call, in a friendly manner, I lay back in the hammock looking up at the cloudless, blue sky. Squinting through the bright sunshine, I closed my eyes and thought about how difficult it was to find the perfect man. Did one actually exist? There were various men in my life, here in Portugal; Mr Hunky who could possibly, only ever be my friend. Andre, the gardener, who strutted about baring his tanned, toned body, but, reminded me I had shoes older than him. Chucky, the flirty pool man, whose adorable wife had become a close and dear friend. Vladimir, the moody handy man, who was quite frankly not my type. What kind of man was I searching for? Was I destined to be forever single? Would I ever meet anyone who lived up to my expectations?

As the summer breeze gently rocked me in my hammock I mulled over my list once again and wondered to myself if this was my stumbling block?

Physical Characteristics.

Tall, at least four inches taller than me. His eyes will be his main feature, they will draw me in with his every look. His hair will be any colour but there will be enough of it to run my fingers through. Body hair is fine as long as it's not a carpet back. No tattoos would be good also, no jewelery other than a watch, which he will always remove in bed. His body will not be skinny, his shoulders will be broad, his belly may have a small pot to match mine. His upper arms will be strong enough to lay my head on at night. His thighs will be those of a rugby player that will enable me to dead leg him with my elbow when he winds me up. His hands will be manly and clean, with a gentle touch. His bottom will be the cutest thing in my world, but not as cute as mine...

Personality

He will ooze confidence with an air of arrogance that he has earned. He will be intelligent and know words that have to be explained to me without making me feel stupid. He will have an organised mind but will be able to throw caution to the wind at a moment's notice. A funny man who always gets the hidden joke. Warm and kind hearted but won't suffer fools gladly. He will know his strengths and yet recognise his weaknesses. He will be honest enough to admit another lady is beautiful but faithful enough not to stray. He will be able to read me like a book without revealing the end...

Status

His employment will be important to him. His salary will afford us a luxurious lifestyle but will not be the most important detail in our relationship. He will come from a large and loving family who will welcome me with open arms. He will have a wide and varied mixture of friends who will become my friends also...

Us

He will always be attracted to me and me him. We will always respect each other's space. We will love each other unconditionally. We will have a mutual trust but both will always have the insight of reasonable doubt. We will strive on a daily basis to work on our relationship without excluding the outside world. And most importantly, he will love my Milo...

My daydreaming suddenly got interrupted by the sound of Ali's new-found toy. Her boom-box. Hearing some familiar tunes blasting out and Ali shouting me to come join her on the trampoline, I pulled myself out of the hammock and wandered over. After much bouncing and plenty of giggles we decided to head off to the market.

Today we were in search of flowers. Ali's daughter was to be married in October and her wedding celebration would be held in the Big Beach house. Ali was determined to push the boat out for this occasion, a marquee the size of a circus tent would be erected in the grounds and flowers were to be adorned everywhere, absolutely everywhere. Pots around the pool, planting in the borders, foliage lining the bridge into the marquee, table flowers, hair flowers, bedroom flowers, you name it, it would have flowers. The lady on the market flower stall had got quite used to our frequent visits. Every week Ali would fill the boot of her car with more flowers, and then spend hours testing out arrangements back at the Big Beach house. It wasn't just flowers to organise. Fairy lights were now popping up everywhere, in the trees, in the bushes, on the fences, through the house. If Milo and Max stood still, they wore fairy lights. And Buddhas, Buddhas appeared all over the garden, big ones, little ones, black ones and white ones. And don't get me started on the fountain; sourced, purchased, delivered, erected and then emptied on a daily basis by Milo and Max. This certainly was going to be the wedding of the century. People would talk of it for years. The Big Beach house would always be known for 'That Wedding'. Just a pity it was not my wedding.

On our way back from the market we stopped off at the Loja Chines; a Chinese warehouse stocking everything under the sun. After rooting through their display of cheap and tacky fake flowers we came across an aisle stocking wild, jungle styled animal masks. The next ten minutes were spent with; Ali wearing a full lion head mask and me in a gorilla one, both jumping out on each other at the end of each aisle. We thought this was hysterical and were both bent double with our laughter. Choosing not to purchase the animal masks, instead we each bought a pair of knickers; with a perfectly placed fake bottom sewn into the seams.

Before heading home, we called at the supermarket to stock up on the weekly groceries, as usual overfilling the trolley and forgetting we were driving the Mouse which was already full of flowers. Once we had managed to stuff all the shopping inside the Mouse, we squeezed ourselves in and chugged home, each holding a pot plant on our laps. Back at the Big Beach house we parked up and placed a large wheelbarrow beside the Mouse. We poured all the shopping into the wheelbarrow and trawled it into the house to be put away. A productive day: Ali and I declared.

Later that evening, as Ali and I were engrossed in another American TV series, Gran did what we call her 'dead impression'. Gran did this quite often. It was rather unnerving. She would stare into a space in the distance, unblinking and appearing to not breathe. Ali and I would exchange glances and silently wonder if this was it? And then, all of a sudden, she would exhale a long, groaning breath and Ali and I would breathe out too.

Bedtime for Gran we decided. And our evening routine began. Ali got the electric wheelchair from the corridor, flicking some tunes onto the boom-box on her way, and we lifted Gran into the chair. As Ali pushed Gran down the corridor to her bedroom, I trailed behind her, Milo and Max both trying to squeeze past in their race to the comfy armchair in Gran's room. Ali was wiggling her bottom, to the tunes blasting out and hadn't realised her trousers had fallen to her ankles, until I squealed out loud at the bird's eye view of her newly purchased fake backside. We were still giggling hysterically as we both lifted Gran into her bed, but Ali had grabbed my leg instead of Grans, at which point I was now practically lying in the bed with Gran. Milo and Max were frantically barking and trying to jump up onto the bed, both thinking this was all some kind of game. Poor Gran just lay there, staring past us, no doubt thinking to herself; she was living with Patsy and Eddie from Ab Fab.

I think Ali and Mee are a crazy pair at times, they're always up to some kind of mischief. And giggle, my word they don't half giggle a lot, they're like naughty school children. How they get away with being the supposed 'responsible adults' in the house amazes me, I think Max and I are more grown up than them. Unless of course we're racing, when Max and I race we are the crazy kids in town. I've nearly perfected the race to Gran's comfy armchair, I just need to get to grips with those pesky slippery corners: they get me every time. The race around the garden is where I come out tops. I can practically fly up and over the wall beside the terrace and then I look back at Max, with his short dumpy legs, bouncing up and down below me. Now that, makes me giggle, just like Ali and Mee.

Chapter 19

An extra special day lay ahead for me. Today my sister Pip and her partner were coming to visit the Big Beach house for a whole week. The Big Beach house welcomed a constant stream of visitors, its doors always open, its belly always full of friends, family or paying guests. But this time the visitors were mine, and Milo looked forward to being spoilt rotten by two people who loved him nearly as much as I did.

I picked them up from Lisbon airport in Ali's car. Now quite a dab hand at this route, having driven Mr Hunky here on numerous occasions, I arrived in quick time. Driving back to the Big Beach house I filled them in on all I'd been up to so far and excitedly spent the journey planning our week ahead. In preparation for the wedding part of our week was to be spent painting. I had promised Ali that we would repaint all the white walls around the pool area and also the large and imposing electric gates into the property. I promised them the sun would shine whilst we did all this painting and that I would provide a constant supply of beers. They both seemed happy enough with this.

During their stay we did manage a few days sightseeing the local area. A day spent exploring Obidos medieval town, a sightseeing bus tour of Lisbon city, a drive out to Peniche for some surfer spotting, and of course a daily walk with Milo down at the lagoon. They both loved the lagoon as much as I did; the tranquil atmosphere it provided to just sit and let life float by, all the while knowing, just beyond the sandbank, the gigantic waves were crashing, relentless upon the shore. They both now understood my fixation with the lagoon.

My little world here in Portugal enchanted them both. Yet, all the while I was enchanted by theirs. They were so in love, so happy with each other, content to be anywhere in world as long as they were together. I wanted that.

Pip and her partner especially loved the evenings at the Big Beach house. After one of our sumptuous evening meals, taken at the big table on the veranda, we all wandered to the bottom garden to take up residence around the sunken fire pit and toast our marshmallows. Seated on our tree stumps, the Caipiroska cocktails began to kick in and I had an urge to start singing Kumbaya my Lord.

Thankfully my singing was bridled as Pip took centre stage reminiscing about her past. She told the story of how she had met her current partner; originally, they had been teenage sweethearts, during the year of 1981, but their romance had dramatically ended; this dramatic end had occurred around the time that they were caught, by our local police constable, in a somewhat compromising situation, whilst trespassing at a local caravan site. PC Plod had informed our parents, who were dismayed by this embarrassment and forbid Pip to continue her romance. Pip was distraught and decided, in typical teenage fashion, to run away from home. It was late in the evening and our parents were in the kitchen, discussing an appropriate punishment for Pip, when I saw her sneaking out of our bedroom; with her boyfriend teddy bear under her coat and wearing her white, tasselled cowboy boots. She made me swear not to snitch on her as she crept down the staircase, tiptoeing past the kitchen door and out of the house. I swore I would not snitch on her: because I was going with her.

Pip and I ran off, into the night, down the dimly lit streets and out of the village. We kept walking, now on pitch black country lanes, not knowing where we were headed and all the while Pip blubbering into her teddy bear, crying for her lost love. With hindsight I can see Pip was having an over the top, defiant, teenage outburst and was running away to punish my parents. Me; I was on an adventure, excited to be included in this drama and was looking forward to the magnificent journey which surely lay ahead.

It rained, it rained heavily and it was dark. I was wearing my thin, school anorak and was soaked to the bones. Pips white cowboy boots were now a muddy brown colour, which just led her to cry even more. We had walked about four miles and not a single car had passed us on the dark and foreboding lanes. I was cold, I was hungry and I needed the toilet. The magnificent journey I had foreseen, was nothing of the sort. Nobody even knew we had run away.

Our journey ended in the next village, where we found a telephone box, inserted a few two pence pieces, and telephoned our parents to please come and collect us. My parents included me in Pip's punishment and we were both grounded, without pocket money, for a whole month.

Over thirty years later Pip had been scrolling through Facebook and had come upon her teenage sweetheart. And the rest is history, as they say. Two people, very much in love and who are meant to be together.

I made a mental note to re-check my Facebook account for any of my childhood sweethearts, who may now be available. But then I remembered I had been an ugly duckling and had never had a childhood sweetheart.

All too soon the time had arrived for them to leave the Big Beach house. Milo seemed to sense their departure, as he sat between them on the garden bench, seemingly lapping up a large supply of hugs before they left. He had loved their visit, he had even ventured into the pool during their stay, albeit floating on the Lilo on top of Pip: not quite in the water.

Our goodbyes were tearful, and once again Pip reiterated, she would always be there for me, always.

Preparations were now coming into full swing for the October wedding at the Big Beach house. With only weeks to go there seemed, still, so much to organize; I did wonder if Ali would pull this off. Her enthusiasm was in overdrive and her ideas were getting crazier by the day. We managed to curtail her plans for fire-eaters and juggling dwarfs during the reception, but we did agree with her on having a Saxophonist playing, whilst the guests mingled around the garden. This wedding could quite easily turn into a circus with some of Ali's crazy ideas.

On a daily basis, hordes of people were now turning up at the Big Beach house, all offering some form of assistance with the wedding preparations. Milo and I were so used to being on our own, prior to arriving in Portugal, that this chaos proved quite overwhelming at times. I missed my Beast so much, I missed that feeling of just closing the door and shutting the world out, safe inside the Beast - Milo and Me. I tended to compensate this feeling by jumping in the Mouse and driving off, spending hours down at the lagoon. Just Milo and Me, sadly minus the Beast.

This week has been fantastic. Pip arrived with the Welsh Man. Oh I've missed them so much since we arrived in Portugal, Pip gives the best hugs and the Welsh Man throws a great ball. The Welsh Man and I have a special bond: we were both born not far from each other in a village in North Wales. Although, I'm a bit miffed with him, as he has now renamed me Chunk. He tells me I'm looking fat, but Clarice disagrees. They did all spend a lot of time painting the walls around the pool area which was quite boring to watch. They also spent a lot of time in the swimming pool, which was rather annoying, but I conquered this one by jumping in and landing on top of Pip floating on a Lilo, she did shriek rather loudly but everyone else was laughing. I've loved having them here and I was so sad to see them leave. Mee seemed pretty upset too, she has had a sad look in her eyes since they left and I don't know how to console her. Even my squeaky yawn isn't working on her. I don't know how I make that noise, it just occasionally pops out as a high-pitched squeal when I yawn and it always make Mee laugh. But not recently.

Chapter 20

The big wedding was imminent. Guests were arriving daily, either staying in the Big Beach house or nearby. My spirits were lifted because Ali's niece, my best friend Sue, had arrived to stay for the week of the wedding. Even though the Big Beach house was bursting at the seams with people, Sue and I could always find a quiet corner, cracked open a bottle of wine, and poured our hearts out to each other. Sue and I truly were best friends; we could go months without any contact and then just pick up where we left off.

Sue and I had an abundance of tasks to keep us busy over the next few days; flower arranging, bed making, meal preparations, shopping, and any other last-minute forgotten wedding details.

The big tent took two whole days to be erected, involving a large mechanical crane and a crew of six men: it was massive job. But, once the inside had been meticulously decorated, it looked beautiful; delicate shimmering drapes floated from the ceiling pooling onto the plush carpeted flooring below, balloons wrapped in twinkly fairy lights danced from crisp white linen-clothed tables, and an array of colourful, freshly scented flowers adorned the room; romance filled the air inside the big tent.

Another one of Ali's wonderful wedding ideas came in the form of a Flash mob dance. Her idea consisted of; about a dozen of her chosen guests would secretly rehearse this Flash mob dance prior to the wedding and then on the day of the wedding, with everyone gathered outside the church and the bride and groom surrounded by their guests, we 'the secret dozen', would, upon hearing the sound of the music blaring from Ali's boom-box, suddenly, without rhyme nor reason, burst into our dance routine to the delight of the unsuspecting crowd. Unfortunately, our rehearsal had amounted to about twenty minutes of nothing but chaos and confusion. I did wonder if we could carry it off?

The Big Beach house now bulged at the seams with wedding guests, a fantastic mixture of Scottish and Portuguese, from both sides of the family. Every bedroom now occupied to full capacity, every couch now a bed.

Milo, who normally barks at anyone who arrives at the house, had given up on this activity choosing to spend most of his days taking refuge on my bed. Max, on the other hand, loved all the commotion and ran about lapping it up. I muddled on amongst the chaos as best I could, making sure I took time out with regular cuddles on the bed with Milo. Just gently stroking his soft velvet ears always helped calm my nerves. It was going to be a crazy few days.

And then finally it was upon us. The actual wedding day. Let the magic begin.

Being the first person to wake in the Big Beach house that morning, I crept into the kitchen, tiptoeing past the bodies on the couches, and quietly brewed a pot of coffee whilst preparing Milo's breakfast. Milo, softly, padded in behind me, had a little sniff on his way past all the bodies, rooted through a few handbags and then ate his breakfast; in his usual ferocious manner.

I took my coffee out to the garden, and sat with Milo, on the bench, absorbing the quiet before the storm. The skies were the clearest of blue and the sun was rising behind the Big Beach house like a big ball of honeycomb. A gentle breeze rustled through the tall palm trees and the voices of the early morning fishermen drifted up from the lagoon. I padded, barefoot, across the neatly cut lawns down towards the marquee, passing numerous little Buddha statues, all smiling up at me. I stood on the quaint wooden bridge leading into the marquee and looked back up at the Big Beach house. The sheer whiteness of the house blinded me and teased me with an image of the Big Beach house wearing its own fluffy white wedding dress. What a perfect setting for a wedding, I thought to myself.

My tranquil moment was interrupted by the sound of people rising from their slumber. I finished my coffee and headed back inside to prepare Gran's first feed.

Gran would not be able to attend the church ceremony, Gran was unable to leave the house these days. But today she would have her hair done and she would wear her Sunday best clothes. She would have a stream of visitors all day, who would each, in turn, sit with her. As I was relieved of my Gran duties for the rest of the day, I took this opportunity to sit next to her bed and tell her all about the wedding day dramas about to unfold. She mostly looked past me, but occasionally she looked me in the eye, as if hearing what I said. At ninety years of age I'm pretty sure she'd had her fair fill of wedding day antics.

The sleepy house was now a buzz of activity as bodies crawled from their beds, caterers arrived, and a small team of hair and beauty technicians set up shop in the dining room. The queue for a 'hair-up' was a long one so I decided a quick wash and blow dry, done by myself, would suffice. Sue agreed with this and suggested we take this opportunity to sneak out in the Mouse for a quiet coffee at the beach café. I readily agreed.

But our sneaky escape didn't last long, as we were both bombarded with text messages of various requests; to pick up more croissants, to locate a missing guest, to dress the electric gates in ribbon and to stop at the chemist for a supply of hangover remedies.

By late morning we were all finally ready to head to the church. Cars filled with guests and drivers were allocated. I was an allocated driver, thankfully not in the Mouse. Milo and Max did attempt to climb into the car with us, but as cute as they looked; Milo wearing his red, silk tie and Max sporting a little black dickie bow, they were to stay at the Big Beach house with Clarice.

The little church in Nadadouro overflowed with well-dressed wedding guests. I peeped through the big wooden church door and seeing there was standing room only, I wandered over to the band stand in the square, where I had spotted Mr Hunky.

"Nicci, you look beautiful my darling, as ever." He said, staring me up and down with a twinkle in his eye.

I was wearing a bright yellow halter neck dress, backless and sitting just slightly above my knee – the permitted length for a fifty something year old woman, I had read somewhere - I had on a pair of classy, peep toe high heels and had even made the effort to paint my nails. My summer bronzed skin had been scrubbed, buffed and moisturised and my hair had been treated to a shimmer conditioning treatment.

Mr Hunky was still staring me up and down as I thought to myself; you don't look so bad yourself, whilst admiring his expensive dark blue suit, crisp white shirt and smart leather shoes. The absence of socks seemed to add to his sexy ensemble.

Mr Hunky handed me a cold bottle of beer from the ice box by his feet and slipped his arm around my waist. We did make a handsome pair. After all the bucks fizz I'd already consumed, a few more of these beers and who knows what might happen today? I thought to myself.

The church service seemed to go on forever, but then as the church bells began to ring the big wooden doors flew open and out flowed the bride and groom. They made a beautiful couple, the joy on their faces was mesmerising. Everyone cheering and throwing confetti at the couple and the crowd seemed to engulf them. I had wandered back to the band stand and had just accepted another beer from Mr Hunky when I heard the music.

"Shit! I have to go." I shrieked at Mr Hunky, pushing my beer into his hand.

I could see, from my elevated position, the 'secret dozen' beginning their flash mob dance. Except the dozen was only ten. I forced myself through the crowd, grabbing Sue, who was having a sly cigarette under the bandstand, and we arrived mid performance to join in with a most disjointed, uncoordinated display of chaos. But, we all, kind of, pulled it off. Nobody watching knew what we were actually supposed to be doing anyway, so they all just happily clapped and cheered us along.

The bride and groom were now leaving the square, I could see various guests trying to squash metres of fabric from the bride's wedding dress into a tiny yet classy two-seater open top sports car, generously donated by Mr Hunky. This romantic journey, taking in the dramatic views of the coastline, with the handsome groom driving and the brides veil blowing in the breeze, would all be captured on film, by the drone above following them.

Everyone had now arrived back at the Big Beach house and as I walked down the steps towards the pool, surveying the array of guests basking in the sunshine - champagne flutes in hand, the sound of the saxophonist drifting above the chatter, and handsome waiters, floating trays of champagne from guest to guest, I thought to myself, 'Damn, I wish I hadn't talked Ali out of booking naked waiters'.

The wedding celebrations were in full swing now, a wondrous atmosphere floated through the big marquee. Speeches were made, food served and alcohol flowed. Being the light-weight drinker that I am, I was beginning to feel the effects of all the alcohol I had consumed so far. I staggered back to the house and took a moment to curl up with Milo on my bed. Although, my moment was possibly longer than that, because when I returned to the marquee, it appeared, I had missed various servings of food and they were now serving the sweets. I managed to persuade the waitress to give me three servings of sweet dishes and wolfed them down just before Sue returned from the free bar, with yet more vodka.

With the bright orange sun setting in the distance behind the marquee, the evening sky set the fairy lights into action. Before long the garden became a twinkle of delight and it felt as if the big moon shone down on only us. People were dancing; dancing in the marquee, dancing in the garden and even dancing in the swimming pool. I was feeling good, so good in fact, I decided now would be a good time to go and find Mr Hunky.

I zigzagged through all the dancing bodies, scanning for his face in the crowd but I couldn't see him anywhere. I carried on searching but he seemed to have disappeared into thin air. He certainly wasn't in the marquee or the garden, so I headed up to the house. Just as I was about to give up my search, I spotted him as I walked through the kitchen corridor. The door to the linen room swung open revealing Mr Hunky, who, through my beer goggles, appeared even more handsome than normal. I stepped forward and was just about to launch myself into his arms, when I faltered. I stood back and watched, as he slowly turned his head and smiled back at a dishevelled, flustered, beautiful young bridesmaid coming out of the linen room behind him. My launch sequence was put on permanent pause.

So many people. They're everywhere. It's like living in a hotel. I've given up on barking to let Mee know every time someone new arrives; my voice is too hoarse. Max seems to be loving all this commotion, I, on the other hand,

114

am missing my peace and quiet. The only bonus is all the food, Clarice is in overdrive and is cooking 24 hours a day.

This morning Mee looked a bit different, her dress was so yellow it looked like a hi-vis vest and she really struggled to walk in those silly shoes. Every time I went in for a cuddle she screeched 'don't slobber on my outfit!'. In comparison, my outfit was rather fetching; a long, silk, red tie. I enjoyed wearing that tie and all the guests took to calling me 'the English gentleman'. I liked that title, it made me feel rather stately.

I didn't see much of Mee for the rest of the day, there was far too much chaos occurring for a gentleman of my calibre to mingle with the crowds, so I chose to remain in my room. Mee did come and visit me later in the day, she just kind of flopped onto the bed and lay there, very still, for ages. That was pretty annoying because she was lying right on my tie and I couldn't budge her off it. I do hope Clarice can launder those creases out.

Chapter 21

With the wedding over the massive clearing up process had begun. Milo and Max were in their element, scavenging the discarded food scattered all over the garden. My head pounded, as I surveyed the carnage that lay before me. This clear up would take days.

Over the coming days, all of the guests gradually left the Big Beach house and once again it was just me, Ali and Gran. We were all on a downer. Even the weather had turned miserable. The blue skies turned grey and it rained heavily nearly every day. Ali was now feeling redundant with no more wedding planning to organise and took it upon herself to arrange a vacation, to New York. She certainly deserved it.

With Summer over, our trips to the market now found me buying warm winter jumpers, and as most of the bustling cafés I had frequented were now closing for winter I spent most days indoors. Every evening we lit the big log burner fire and sat on our couches, wrapped in cosy blankets, eating crisps and chocolate and watching Netflix. The Paying Guests upstairs were dwindling and the Big Beach house grew quieter day by day. Each long day seemed to be drifting into another. I was just plodding along and this was making me feel anxious. I was also experiencing a feeling of home sickness, even though I didn't actually have a home to miss.

While Ali was busy planning her trip to New York, I got busy with thoughts of planning my future. Portugal had been good to me but it hadn't entirely satisfied my appetite. I still had a yearning for true love, for that one special man who could help me create my happy ever after. And, I missed the Beast; being out on the open road, driving unknown paths and creating a journey of discovery and adventure. I felt I was ready to leave Portugal; I just didn't know where I wanted to go. I needed to figure out if I was running away from something or running towards it. I felt convinced that if I found the right man, I would be happy, but I also knew that I didn't actually *feel* unhappy at present. Why couldn't I settle? Why couldn't I accept what I had and stop chasing a dream? Why did I have to constantly search for something else? But then I reminded myself, that this is what life is about; we are programmed for three basic instincts; food, shelter and love. I was only doing what came naturally: looking for all three.

I decided to call upon my good old friend Gumtree. Gumtree had been good to me in the past; providing me with the purchase of the Beast and for helping sell most of my worldly possessions. I sat down one evening and wrote out an advertisement to place on-line. And this is what I wrote:

My name is Nicci I am a single, fifty-year-old woman and Milo is my four-year-old fox red Labrador. We are looking to house sit, baby sit, granny sit, any kind of sit!

We are currently in Portugal caring for 90-year-old Gran, who has dementia. We also help out with running of the guest house. Previous to this we travelled around Scotland and Ireland in our motor-home. During our travels I wrote a blog which attracted a fair amount of media attention.

We are returning to the UK soon and my desire is to write. I am hoping to find a house sit in the UK where I can possibly live in my motor-home with Milo and pursue my writing. A rural location is our desire, plus we love beaches.

I am an extremely self-sufficient person, extremely tidy and organised and tend to deal with whatever life throws at me!

I'm happy to consider short term or long term although would prefer long term. I'm happy to consider any possibilities; however whacky they may be!

I added a selection of appropriate photographs of Milo, Me and the Beast and then hit publish. I didn't quite know what I was hoping to achieve but felt I had nothing to lose. For a few days nothing happened, no responses, no replies. Then, one day I noticed a reply in my in-box. I felt quite excited that someone had replied, that is, until I read it; a rather enthusiastic gentleman requiring a lady to provide him with a weekly massage for a nominal fee. He even stated that he would be quite happy for this 'massage' to take place in my motor-home. This was not the type of whacky I had considered.

I felt despondent. I'd also noticed my advertisement had been placed directly underneath another one advertising 'Gangster for Hire'. This 'gangster' stated his location as Holloway and offered his services as; *will consider any bank job, post office, house breaking, top of the range motors – have a life time's experience.* His main credential being he'd never grassed in his life. Maybe I should contact him? I thought, a little intrigued. We could hook up as a modern-day Bonnie and Clyde?

With Ali now in New York it was just me, Gran and the dogs left in the Big Beach house. I hadn't seen much of Mr Hunky, not since he'd come out the closet, and even though he'd now had his driving licence reinstated, he had kindly let me keep the Mouse. On Clarice days I would go off in the Mouse, park up on the cliffs at the top of Foz, and spend hours staring out to the Atlantic Ocean. Something will turn up, I kept telling myself. 'Life is like a box of chocolates, you never know what you're gonna get'. I just prayed it wouldn't be the yukky coffee cream one.

And then one day, I got another reply to my Gumtree advertisement. And, best of all it appeared to be a genuine one. A gentleman, Mr J, who resided in Northern France, wrote to say he was seeking a live-in help for his teenage son.

The basis of the email told me he lived at home with his son in a rural location of Northern France, his son studied at the local school for the final year of his education. Father and son were both English and father needed to make frequent business trips abroad, leaving his son without care. He went on to tell me his son required minimal care, an occasional lift to school if he missed the bus, car provided, but an adult on the premises would put his mind at rest. I would have my own room in the house, and plenty of free time to explore the whole of Northern France in my motor-home. Milo would be most welcome as they also had a dog, named Bear.

This was definitely not coffee cream. This could possibly be my chocolate fudge. The photographs he'd attached in his email, showed me his quaint French style house, surrounded by countryside and near to the town of Mortagne au Perche. All my expenses would be covered and if I was interested in this position, he would fly over to Portugal and interview me. I now had a feeling of excitement for my future; my next adventure was in the making.

Ali had returned from New York and as she excitedly told me all about her adventure, I listened intently, all the while wondering how I should bring up the news of my imminent departure. I loved Ali to bits and living with her had been good for my soul, but I needed to explain why I wanted to leave.

"It's not you, it's me." sounded like a breakup with a boyfriend.

"I'm homesick." made me sound like a child.

"Ali, I need to continue my adventure, with Milo, in the Beast." were the words which I spoke out loud.

"Oh, Nicci, I totally understand, Sweety." Ali said. "I have loved having you live here, you have been my rock where Gran is concerned. But I do understand your desire to move on, you're a spirited soul and you must continue your adventure." Ali was now hugging me and Milo and Max chose to join in.

Two days later I was sitting in a café in Lisbon being interviewed by Mr J. He came across as a lovely little man and my gut instinct told me he was a good person. He seemed happy with my credentials and we both agreed on a trial three-month period, his main concern being the well-being of his son, mine being the hope that my Beast would be up to the journey. We agreed on a start date in early January, giving us both time to enjoy the Christmas festivities with our families.

Ali got straight onto the arrangements for our travel back to the UK. The cheap airline ticket which brought Milo here was a damn sight more expensive for re-entry into the UK. Ali had to jump through all sorts of hoops to organise this return trip.

My last night in Foz do Arelho and I was pretty much organised, although with all the market trips I'd made I did have to borrow an extra suitcase from Ali; for all my excess luggage. Milo on the other hand would leave with exactly the same luggage he had arrived with; his collar and his lead. Milo hadn't looked too happy earlier in the day, when he saw me cleaning out the cargo crate he had travelled over in, he now lay quite still on my bed, watching me struggle to close the lid on my suitcase.

"Hey Milo, guess where we are going tomorrow?" I said enthusiastically.

"We are going to see Pip and the Welsh Man and Philip and my mum. Isn't that exciting?"

His ears pricked up slightly but then drooped back down as he let out a little groan noise. I think he knew *how* we would travel back.

My plans to finish packing and get an early night before our departure were ambushed by Ali and Mr Hunky. They decided we should go down to the hotel on the beach and take in the sunset, with one last Caipiroska. Trouble is one turned into about five and I had to be practically carried back to the Big Beach house by Mr Hunky. Back at the house my head was spinning and I felt nauseous. Ali grabbed me a bucket from the kitchen and Mr Hunky held back my hair whilst I, unglamorously, vomited into the bucket. Mortified, I stumbled down the corridor in search of my room and passed out on my bed. But then I was rudely awakened from my comatose state, by Mr Hunky, lying on top of me, his lips locked onto mine.

"What the heck!" I spluttered, pushing him off me.

"Ah, Nicci! You are alive!" He exclaimed. "I give you the life of kiss, I have saved you."

Who says romance is dead? I thought, as Milo jumped onto the bed and sniffed at my hair.

I've got a sick feeling in the pit of my stomach. Mee tells me we are returning to the UK. Now, that, I am excited about. But the way we will return is what terrifies me. I saw her cleaning that crate today, the one they put me in last time. Which confirms my worst dread: we are flying home. I've been trying to give myself those pep talks, the one's Mee always gives herself; 'I'll be fine' 'I've done it before, I can do it again' 'What's the worst that can happen?' But I still feel sick.

The best bit is we will be staying with the family for Christmas, which basically equals food, lots of it. I will miss Portugal though, especially Ali. And of course; my annoying little adopted brother Max, plus Gran, Clarice and of course the beach. What I won't miss, here in Portugal, is the lack of socks. There aren't any. I love to find random, smelly socks, I can sniff them out anywhere and Mee always chases me when I get one. But for some reason Mee hasn't worn any since we've been here, she is always bare footed. I wonder if she will wear any in France? Because France, she tells me, is to be our next adventure.

Chapter 22

Our return journey to Manchester was just as traumatic as the outbound one. In fact, it probably felt worse because we knew what lay ahead. The day began with me waking up to the smell of vomit in my hair, I'd only had about 3 hours of drunken sleep and there was no time to wash it before our early morning departure. During the drive to Lisbon airport, Ali and I were both very quiet, we were both feeling a little sad. I spent the journey reflecting on how wonderful Portugal had been, my adventure had provided some wonderful memories and I'd made so many new friends whilst living a somewhat idyllic lifestyle. Ali and I had been like sisters, enjoying so many girly giggles during the months with all our mischievous antics. She had also managed to enjoy the luxury of having some well-deserved Ali time, whilst entrusting the care of Gran to me. We were truly going to miss each other so very much.

We arrived at the airport, and as instructed, made our way to the Cargo area. When we had first arrived in Portugal, Milo's weight, for his crate, had been 27 kilos. He now hit the scales at nearly forty kilos. 'Oh Clarice', I thought. Luckily, the man checking our documents didn't seem to notice this discrepancy, lucky because the price increments per kilo were extortionate. Milo, reluctantly, entered his crate and I, once again, turned into a bubbling wreck. Ali tried to console me, telling me not to worry. Milo would be fine and it was only two hours before he would be so excited to see his family. But I knew Milo would be even more terrified this time, as he would have the memory of his journey out here embedded into his brain. I spoke my usual 'I'm just going to the shops, Baby, I won't be long, Baby, I love you.' knowing this was of little comfort and I would no doubt be blamed again for his two hours of hell. I now had to make my way to the terminal building, leaving Milo in the care of the cargo staff, until we would be reunited in Manchester.

Once I had checked in for my flight, Ali and I hugged, and hugged, and hugged. Her, telling me if France turned out to be the wrong decision, I was close enough to drive the Beast straight over to Foz do Arelho. Me, promising that I would do so.

I felt fretful for the entire flight, having moments of panic that the airline might have boarded Milo onto the wrong aircraft and he could now be travelling to Latin America or Brazil. Eventually I arrived in Manchester and my son, Philip, was there to meet me; looking even more handsome than ever. I admired him in wonderment, hearing Ali's voice when talking of her own son; 'my creation' she would say so often. And here was mine. "My creation." I exclaimed as I threw my arms around his neck and told him how much I had missed him.

"Woah, Mum! You smell of sick." He said pushing me away.

We climbed into Philips car and drove off high-speed to the Cargo area to collect Milo. I jumped out of the car and bounced through the office door, disregarding all other customers, and shouted out "I'm here to collect Milo". And there he was, behind the desk, sitting quite contentedly, at the feet of the cargo man - being fed biscuits.

"He's a cracker, this one." said the jolly cargo man. "Can we keep him?" He laughed.

"Er, No." I said, my bottom lip slightly quivering. Milo hadn't even acknowledged my presence and had not taken his eye off the biscuit in cargo man's hand.

Milo, eventually, having eaten all the biscuits, came outside, did his business, made a fuss of Philip and then fell asleep on the back seat of the car. I was, it appeared, once again receiving the silent treatment as my punishment.

Back at mum's house we had a lovely family meal, a good old catch-up and then I fell into bed for some much-needed sleep. We only had a few days to prepare the Beast for our adventure to France.

Well to be honest that wasn't quite as bad as I had expected. I think I'd wound myself up so much prior to the journey that I was exhausted when they put me into that crate. Quite frankly I was more concerned when they put me on those weighing scales. Welsh Man might have actually been right in naming me Chunk. I made a decision, that once Christmas was out of the way I would concentrate on losing some weight: Said no Labrador, ever! Haha!

Mee was her usual hysterical self on leaving me and went about promising me the usual biscuits after the 'shop'. You know, if I didn't know better, I'd think she spent her whole life at the 'shops'.

When they let me out of the crate a very nice man gave me some very nice biscuits. I was that engrossed in these tasty biscuits that I didn't notice Mee at first. But then I heard her; screeching my name across the room and then practically throwing herself over the counter towards me. All rather embarrassing to be honest. Once I'd made sure there were no more biscuits on offer, I walked outside to the welcome sight of one of the saner members of our family, Philip.

Milo and Me at the lagoon Foz do Arelho

Milo and Me frolicking beside the Atlantic Ocean

Chapter 23

Christmas came and went, and the best present I got was my Beast. I felt so happy to have him back in my life, he'd spent the last few months tucked up in a garage and thankfully appeared to be in good condition. Now preparations began for his journey to France; deflectors on his headlights, GB sticker on his rear, a breakdown triangle, two hi-vis vests - one for me, one for Milo and a breathalyser kit in the glove box (just one - for me). All the necessaries for travel abroad were duly taken care of. I even added European RAC breakdown cover, just in case.

My suitcases of summer clothes I'd brought back from Portugal were safely stored in Mum's spare room and my winter clothes were now stuffed into the tiny wardrobe inside the Beast. My kitchen cupboard bulged with my essential food items mainly consisting of coffee, chocolate and crisps. All bedding and blankets were washed and tumble dried, all the interior dusted and polished. We spent an afternoon at Wirral Small Cars, where they declared the Beast, once again, fit to travel.

I had our Tunnel ticket, which for some unknown reason, had printed on the first page - 'Pets - Dog/Cat/Ferret'. I definitely did not book these extra animals but as long as Dog was included, I didn't mind. Milo's vet check proved to be quite straight-forward, having done most of the ground work prior to our Portugal trip.

So, all in all, we were ready for our adventure. France, oooh la la! I'd been on Google and had been pleasantly surprised to read that French men were considered the holy grail of international lovers and sex was something of a national sport for French men. I was more than willing to confirm if this was in fact true.

Yet again my family were taking me to a local restaurant for another goodbye meal, I'm sure they were getting fed-up waving me off, or maybe they were fed-up with me returning? Anyway, I made sure I told them how grateful I was for their constant support and encouragement, during, what my mum still referred to as, my mid-life crisis.

And we're off! I'd allowed myself four days travel to reach Mr J's house and had booked some overnight stops en-route, through the Caravan and motor-home Club. Milo seemed quite excited to be, once again, in the Beast and had settled right back into his usual spot, on the couch behind my driver seat, head resting on my shoulder.

We spent the first leg of our journey mostly at a standstill, on the M6 motorway. I had been tempted to put the kettle on and make a pot of coffee at one point. A few hours later and we had only progressed as far as the M1 motorway. The Beast was tiring and Milo was getting restless, so I started looking for a suitable safe place to park-up. Our safe place turned out to be a fairly well-lit car-park beside a restaurant in Hemel Hempstead, having checked with the proprietor that we would not be wheel clamped overnight.

The next morning, after a run in the local park for Milo and a pot of hot coffee for me, we continued our journey towards Folkestone. Whilst driving over the Dartford crossing, and making a mental note to ask Pip if she would kindly pay my crossing fee, I noticed a light flickering on my dashboard. It looked like my battery light, but in the bright winter sunshine I couldn't be sure. If I squinted my eyes it looked lit up, if I opened them wide it looked unlit. After a few miles I pulled into a service station and sat, with the engine running, trying to decide if the light was on or off. It felt like I was glaring at a pregnancy testing stick and having Googled my symptoms I now decided the Beast was definitely pregnant. Pregnant with either a faulty alternator, failing battery or corroded wires.

Google also informed me this 'pregnancy' could affect the on-board electrics, so I made the decision to drive on towards my camp site using as few electrics as possible; lights and wipers remained on due to the awful weather conditions, radio and heaters were turned off and blankets were wrapped around me and Milo for the remainder of the route.

As soon as we arrived at our camp-site, The Black Horse Farm, I telephoned the RAC. I think I may have misled them slightly with my garbled information – female, alone, vulnerable and pregnant - because they were with me in no time. The RAC man pulled up in front of the Beast - I was daydreaming about a story I had read somewhere about a woman falling in love and marrying her RAC man - when he tapped on my driver window and brought me back to reality.

The diagnosis was indeed a faulty alternator, but not terminal. We settled in to our camp-site and took advantage of the on-site 'dog walk path' which pleased Milo. Being the only motor-home parked up we also had the full run of the area around us, which, to Milo's delight, held an abundance of bunny rabbits. After a delicious meal of rabbit stew, I mean sausage and mash, we settled in for a good night's sleep before our Channel crossing in the morning.

The next morning, I was woken by the extreme quietness. The kind of quietness that makes you wonder if you have suddenly gone deaf overnight. I threw back my duvet, as usual whacking my knuckles on the ceiling, and climbed down my ladder out of bed. I padded to the back door, Milo at my heels, and having lifted all my catches, opened the door. And there before me I saw the reason for the quietness. Snow. Lots of it. A full thick carpet of whiteness lay before me. Milo bounced out the door, sank into about a foot of snow and proceeded to do his impersonation of a snow plough. He zigzagged through the field, nose down, snorting up little sprays of snow as he did so. Hmm, I thought, I wonder how the Beast will cope driving in this thick snow?

Driving in thick snow was not the Beast's first problem that day. Starting his engine was. Having packed up, ready to leave, I put the key in the ignition and got absolutely nothing. So, I put on my wellies and plodded up to the reception area to ask for help. Help came in the form of the lovely manager and his tractor. Jump leads were attached and numerous attempts were made to start the engine. The engine would not start. I was going nowhere.

Once again, the RAC came to my rescue. Considering the atrocious weather, once again they were with me in no time. Having managed to start the engine the RAC man now informed me that my alternator most definitely needed replacing, it would not get me to France. He then telephoned a local garage who said they could fit me in this morning and replace my alternator. The nice RAC man kindly suggested I follow his van, in the Beast, to said garage in Folkestone. So off we skidded.

I spent the whole morning sat inside the Beast, parked up on the garage forecourt, watching the staff manoeuvre cars in and out of extremely tight spaces, whilst I waited for the delivery of my new alternator. My only entertainment came in the form of random displays of snow ball fights, between the staff on the forecourt. I'd messaged Mr J and he had kindly changed my euro tunnel ticket to a later departure time.

After a few more hours, my new alternator finally arrived and the mechanic proceeded to fit it into the engine of the Beast. I sat in my driver seat nervously watching this take place, to me it was like watching open heart surgery on a loved one. The mechanic struggled at times and had to call for assistance from his colleagues, Milo and I sat up front, holding our breath, silently praying the Beast would pull through. And he did, although I can't say the same for my credit card. I paid the bill and then messaged Mr J, who once again changed my euro tunnel ticket to an even later departure time.

Eventually we were ready to leave the garage, but having viewed the only exit out of the garage, which was an extremely tight alley between two buildings, I knew I would struggle manoeuvring the Beast out in reverse. But, having witnessed the ease in which the staff performed these manoeuvres I politely asked for help. One of the overly eager snow ball fighters jumped into my driver seat, declaring this would be no problem, love. And it wasn't a problem, until he had to swing my rear end into the road at the end of the narrow alley. "Blooming heck, this steering is tight love!" He declared, as he violently turned and turned my steering wheel full lock. "It has no power steering" I screamed back at him, whilst watching the plastic, covering the neck of the wheel, crack and splinter over the dashboard. Ignoring me, he continued, with both hands, using all the muscle power he could muster, to force my steering wheel into a full lock, with a look of utter determination on his face. I could hear the neck of the steering column creaking under this force and I suddenly realised that this man had no knowledge of how to drive a vehicle without power steering.

When he had eventually reversed the Beast into the road he pulled up, half on the pavement half on the road and proceeded to jump out the door.

"You can't leave it like that!" I said, observing the bits of plastic lying on the floor and the wiring inside of the steering column, now in full view.

"I'll be back in a minute." He said and ran off.

He returned with a roll of black gaffer tape and I watched as he aggressively wrapped the whole roll around my steering column, leaving a small gap for the ignition key.

"There you go, sorted." And he was gone.

I sat there, staring in dismay at the carnage before me. I managed to peel back some tape and fit the key into the ignition. I started the engine, peeled some more tape away from my indicator arm and edged forward into the oncoming traffic. I so wanted to go back into the garage and kick up a stink about what had just happened, but I was now in panic mode. I had already missed three departure times on my tunnel crossing, I didn't want to miss another. So, I nervously drove through the confusing town-centre one-way system, all the while wondering if my steering wheel might drop off.

We finally arrived at the tunnel crossing just in time for our departure. The man at the gate confirmed our booking and asked where I was travelling to. I told him I was going to a camp-site in Calais and from the look on his face I wondered if he thought I meant the refugee camp-site.

Boarding the train was a weird experience. I don't know what I expected but it literally was a 'train'. A large side door glided open and I drove the Beast from the platform, through the door and into the inside of the brightly lit carriage. Following the other, mainly smaller vehicles, we all slowly edged down the train, until instructed to stop. Further instructions were then given for engines off and handbrakes on. A member of staff checked that my gas bottle had been switched to the off position and told me I was allowed to leave the vehicle and stretch my legs if I so wished. I declined. I did not wish to leave my Beast. As the train departed, the motion of movement, added with the knowledge of how much water sat above us, unnerved me slightly. I chose to sit in the back of the van, on the couch cuddled up with Milo, who looked slightly confused that the Beast was moving, but I was not in the driver seat.

Within about thirty minutes we had reached our destination. We were in Calais – now very late and very dark. I'd had the foresight to pre-load the sat-nav with the address of our pre-booked camp-site, Camping Bal, and also, I'd updated my settings from miles to kilometres, so as not to confuse me. My sat-nav lady began to issue me with my directions, with some endearing pronunciations, and before long I'd left the main road and was headed down a long and winding country road. Although I had driven quite confidently on the left in Portugal, it had been in a left-hand drive car, now I was driving on the left and sitting on the right, not so easy in the Beast.

Having eventually found the camp-site, woken up the owner to let us in, chosen a suitable pitch in the dark and turned off the engine, I could now breathe out. I was in France; Milo, Me and the Beast had made it.

Snow! Oh, I do love a bit of snow. And this was really soft thick snow, my favourite. Mee laughed a lot this morning, every time I ran through the snow, she just burst out laughing. But the laughing stopped. The laughing stopped when the big orange van appeared.

We then spent the rest of the day locked inside the Beast, it was so boring. After hours of just waiting around we were eventually on our way to France. We even travelled on a train, which for me was very similar to the Irish ferry crossing, but this seemed to freak Mee out a bit and she had to come and sit next to me for some Milo reassurance. So, here we are, in France, beginning our next adventure.

Chapter 24

France provided us with a glorious sunrise on day one. The ground glistened with frost, the sky awash with a pink glow and the air sharp and fresh. After a brisk Milo walk and a pot of much needed hot coffee, we were ready to start the drive to Mr J's house in Saint Jouin de Blavou. My sat-nav lady disagreed. She insisted there was no such place and pushed me for alternative addresses. After much frustration I finally figured out that typing 'St' is not the same as typing 'Saint'.

Driving on the motorways in France was pleasant until I reached my first toll. Sitting on the wrong side of the vehicle, with no electric windows and my purse hidden somewhere in the back of my van I began to panic. Having finally found my purse, I jumped out of the van, noting the queuing cars behind the Beast and stood, blankly, in front of the pay machine. I had no idea what to do so I pressed the intercom button for assistance. Obviously, the person at the other end spoke to me in French, and I couldn't understand a word he was saying to me. He soon figured out that I was English and asked me where I had come from. I politely told him I came from Liverpool, because not many people know where the Wirral is. Duh! He didn't want to know where I was born, he wanted to know where I had joined the motorway. The cars originally queued behind me were now all trying to reverse into vacant toll booths, whilst my credit card took another hammering.

Now on country lanes, and enjoying passing through the quaint little villages of Normandy my mood relaxed. I began to feel more comfortable driving with the pavements on my right and was getting quite used to the many cars speeding past me from my left. After a few wrong turns and a fair bit of back-tracking, I finally arrived at my destination. Mr J and his son, Le garçon, were waiting at the door to greet us and guided the Beast into a suitable, safe parking place.

Before stepping out of the Beast, I sat for a moment to collect my thoughts. Although I'd done this many a time before I still always had a mini moment of dread. A single female about to enter the home of a complete stranger would always hold an element of danger. My gut feeling usually told me everything would be OK, but a little voice in my head would often question this. Am I willingly placing myself in a position of danger? If the worst happened would people say 'it's her own fault'? As usual my gut feeling won and grabbing my handbag, I jumped out the van.

Mr J's home was a traditional French long house; downstairs homed a kitchen, living room, toilet, office and storage room and upstairs were two and a half attic bedrooms and a bathroom. The property sat in a large fenced field and Milo immediately went exploring the perimeters and seemed to be in his element. That is until he met Bear. Bear looked like a small German Shepherd dog, aged about one-year old and he was extremely excited to meet Milo. He came bounding across the field towards Milo, eager to play. We were inside the house at this point and Mr J had closed the bottom half of the stable style door. This door did not deter Milo. His usual safety net, the Beast, was not there for him, so he took a long, running jump and shot right through the air like an Olympian hurdler, clearing the stable door and straight into the house, landing at my feet. Luckily, Mr J and Le garçon found this display quite amusing and didn't send us packing there and then.

After a lovely home-cooked meal, wonderful conversation and plenty of wine, Milo and I headed upstairs to our room. Our room was delightful; wooden floorboards, white-washed walls and a big comfy bed, all housed under the eaves. The only window in my room was a small skylight in the roof, which although I couldn't reach, I could look up to the twinkle of a million bright stars shining in the black sky above. I placed Milo's bed next to mine and he happily curled into a ball to sleep, I followed suit, pleasantly surprised to find a warm electric blanket under the sheets.

In the morning, Mr J ran through details of what he roughly required from me; Le garçon needed to be driven into the village each morning to catch the bus to school. If he missed the bus, I would have to drive him to his school, in a car provided by Mr J. I could then do whatever I wished during the day. When Le garçon returned from school, Mr J said Le garçon was more than capable of feeding himself, but if I wished to cook a meal for him, then that would be a bonus. Le garçon seemed to be an extremely mature sixteen-year-old boy and Mr J just wanted reassurance of an adult on the premises when he went away travelling. Mr J would be back and forth to the house and I would be free to go travelling whenever he was back. This all suited me fine.

Later in the day Mr J took me into the local town, Mortagne au Perche, to accustom me with my surroundings. There were plenty of supermarkets, coffee shops and patisseries to keep me happy and Mr J also pointed out some excellent dog walks for Milo. Mr J had organised a visit to a local garage where my Beast's steering column was given a thorough check and thankfully declared safe. That evening we took a drive out to Mr J's local, Le Reveillon Jazz Café, where we bought fresh baguettes from a small table positioned at the door and everyone knew each other. All in all, my local area appeared to provide all that I needed.

Before long, Mr J left for the UK and it was day one of me taking Le garçon to the bus stop. It was all going fine; Le garçon had eventually risen in a typical teenage zombie fashion, had finally found the scattered contents of his school bag and had grabbed half a baguette to eat en-route. We got into Mr J's Mercedes and I started the engine, Le garçon busily scrolled through the radio stations whilst I was desperately trying to find reverse gear. I could not find it. Try as I might it would not go into reverse. Even Le garçon tried, but the car just kept edging forward, towards the garage wall. Eventually, rather than hit the garage wall, I gave up and chose to take the Beast, unfortunately it was now so late we had missed the village bus and I had to drive him all the way to his school. I think Le garçon lost all street cred that morning, arriving at the school gates and stepping out of the Beast in front of his class mates.

Over the coming days I spent most of my time quite content pottering around the house, walking the dogs, doing some writing and learning to speak French. I'd downloaded a how to speak French app and felt pleased when I received a notification informing me, I was now '1% fluent French'. I've got this, I thought to myself.

One day, I decided to pop into town and have a mooch around the local market. Having purchased a few English paperbacks, I was now sitting at a pavement café enjoying a coffee and doing my favourite activity of people watching. And then I saw him. A most handsome and distinguished gentleman seated at the table beside me. He sat reading a book and drinking one of those typically French, tiny cups of coffee, and at his feet lay a straw basket holding fresh flowers and baguettes. I found myself just staring at him, studying his handsome features and imagining what kind of personality he had. I also did that thing; I tried to mirror his behaviour and took my own book out of my bag and pretended to read. But my sly glances over the top of my book told me he hadn't even noticed me. Then to add to my dismay I was approached by a large and somewhat scruffy old lady who sat down at my table, lit up a cigarette and muttered something to me in French. I had no idea what she was saying to me but she had made herself quite comfortable beside me at my table. Then Mr Handsome spoke. In English.

"She is asking if it is okay to rest her legs?" He said in a soft, sensual French accent, resting his book on his lap.

"Oh, oui, oui." I replied, in probably, not such a sensual, Scouse accent.

"You like to read, yes?" He enquired.

"Oh, I do, yes, I do love to read" I gushed, now quite oblivious of my table mate.

"I know of a local book shop that exchanges books for free. English books too, I can give you their address if you wish?" He offered.

"Oh, thank you. Merci, merci beaucoup." I replied, determined to exercise my 1% French fluency.

I watched him intently as he wrote down the address, admiring his fine physique, and noting he was of mixed race, I don't know which race but, in my mind, he certainly won it. He went on to tell me he came to this café every Saturday, at the same time. So of course, me being me, I translated this into a 'date': and fell a little bit in love. But then, as he stood up to leave, and handed me the note, I screamed a little scream inside. From his left hand there glistened a gold band: a wedding ring.

I sat there for a while longer, after he'd left, daydreaming of our future together. In my daydream my Mr Handsome was in fact a lonely widow, and the flowers in his basket were to be placed upon the grave of his dearly departed wife. He continued to wear the wedding ring in memory of her, and also on behalf of their children, who were now all grown-up and wanted him to be happy and in love, once again - with me. Scruffy old lady was now smiling at me and no doubt agreed with my synopsis.

So, the following Saturday I dressed myself up in an outfit befitting a future wife and headed back to the same café to meet my handsome, lonely widow for our 'date'. I spotted him as soon as I arrived, seated at the same table and looking as handsome as I remembered. But as I got closer, I noticed him gently rocking a small child in the pushchair beside him and that he was in a deep and adoring conversation with his very much 'undead' wife. It was too late to turn around and leave, and as he gave me a slight nod of his head, barely acknowledging my presence, I sat down, alone, at another table. I sat there, for what felt like forever, watching him gush over his little family, oblivious to the pain of my broken heart. I did kid myself, for a moment, that maybe his wife was in fact his sister and the child his nephew, and any minute now he would rush over with declarations of his undying love for me. He didn't.

Eventually, I returned to the real world and mused over what Le garçon might like for tonight's dinner.

It's OK this France place. We're in a nice house and we're going on some good walks. Sometimes we have to take that Bear character with us, which is a bit annoying. When Mee throws 'my' ball he tries to race ahead to catch it. Obviously, he rarely gets it before me, but if he does, he just runs off across the field and won't give it back.

Mee went out this morning, looking rather lovely, and chirping on about meeting: the one. Result, I prayed. Maybe now, we can stop all this chaos and live happily ever after? Short lived: she came back in a right strop. It appears her 'married men radar' needs some fine tuning. Oh well, the hunt continues...

Chapter 25

Mr J now back from his business trip meant I had a few days to myself, to go off exploring in the Beast. I decided not to venture too far on our first night away and drove only about an hour away, to a place named Alecon. France is very motor-home friendly, there are Aires all over the place, and usually free of charge. I found a nice little Aire close to the town centre of Alecon and even achieved an hour of free electricity. We spent a couple of days mainly exploring the historic town centre and taking long walks along the Sarthe river, but all too soon the time came for our return to the house.

Back at the house the snow had started falling and the fields were bedecked with white powder. Mr J suggested I store the Beast in the big shed so as not to freeze the pipes. This meant the Mercedes was now parked outside on the road, and the next day Le garçon phoned asking me to collect him from the bus stop in the village. As I revved forward to drive away, I could feel the wheels spinning but the car wasn't moving. Being a rear wheel drive the more I revved the more the car sank further and further into the snow sodden mud. I tried using low revs, back and forth, slight rocking, but all to no avail. Mud was spraying everywhere and I was going nowhere. I even tried putting an old piece of carpet under the rear wheels, but the carpet just buried itself deep into the mud. Le garçon eventually appeared, having walked all the way home, to see me covered from head to toe in mud and with a shovel in my hand. He tried his best to push and dig while I revved, but he also ended up splattered in mud. Eventually we both gave up and Le garçon made a phone call to the local farmer. Help arrived in the form of, first a tractor and then a JCB. The car was eventually pulled out of the mud leaving a rather deep hole just in front of the garage.

The following day, Mr J informed me he was going back to the UK for a few days and would be taking the Mercedes and Le garçon with him. I didn't take it personally.

Later that evening, I decided to take advantage of the empty house and have a nice hot bath. The shower and toilet were downstairs whereas the bathroom was upstairs, tucked under the eaves, between the two bedrooms. I felt more comfortable taking a bath whilst alone in the house, because although the door panels were made of frosted glass, I still felt like I could be seen through this glass. I lay back in the bubbles, looking up at the stars through the sky light, soaking in the warmth of the water. But I had an uncomfortable feeling someone was watching me. I knew there was nobody else in the house, but this unnerving feeling of eyes upon me felt creepy. I sat up, very slowly, and looked towards the door and, at the bottom of the door, where two small square glass panels were missing, I saw two sets of eyes staring right at me. Milo and Bear were lying on the floor outside the door, showing just their heads, squashed through the missing panels, looking right at me. Who knew, voyeur dogs!

After my bath, I decided to have an early night. Having settled Bear downstairs, Milo and I headed up to our room. I was just falling asleep when I heard a very loud scratching noise from the ceiling above my head. I sat bolt upright and turned on the light. The scratching noise continued and Milo was now sitting up and his eyes were following the noise in the ceiling above him. I had no idea what kind of creature was making this noise, but I had a feeling it was a large one. It darted from one corner of the room to another, falling silent for a moment, and then scurrying again through the eaves. I nervously padded around my room looking for any obvious areas that this creature could possibly enter my room from. Having assured myself there were none, I fell into a night of fitful sleep.

I decided to spend the next few days concentrating on writing my book. The fact being, months earlier, I'd been approached by an agency who, having followed my story, wanted to publish a book depicting my adventure. They were so encouraging with their talk, promising me all sorts, even telling me they were flying one of their agents out to Portugal to work with me on said book. Well, this encouraging talk went on for months but then I heard more and more excuses of, "We'll get the ball rolling soon." Soon seemed to get further and further away. Eventually I woke up and smelled the coffee – the publishing world is gut-wrenching. So, I decided to write my book myself. It can't be that hard, can it?...

The Beast, now parked up in a meadow beside the house, provided the perfect writing place for me. The view from my van window across the rolling green fields provided an inspiring and peaceful atmosphere. As long as Milo and Bear had enjoyed their morning walk, I had all day to write, my only interruptions being the occasional tractor passing by. Oh, and my lust for information, the internet has always been my downfall for distraction; 'who's tweeting what today?' 'what is that person on Facebook, who I've never even met, eating for dinner?' 'what does the word Callipygous mean?'. So, after three days of only my own company and not a huge amount of writing done, I now began questioning what I was doing with my life? The what, why and how ran through my mind and had me question everything I'd achieved so far. It was time to seek some guidance. I telephoned Ali in Portugal.

"I'm not achieving anything." I bemoaned to Ali. "I don't know what I'm doing with my life, what should I be doing Ali?"

"Nicci, you are doing what you set your mind to do, Sweety." She told me.

"People might choose to climb Mount Everest, a certain career, or a family life. You have chosen 'this'. This is what you are doing. This is what you have chosen. You are achieving." Ali quite clearly told me. And it made sense, to me. I would continue to decide to do something, and do it. This.

That night, feeling slightly perked up after Ali's conversation, I decided to venture out the house. A café in town, I'd visited during the day, had live jazz music playing and the barman, Climon, told me I'd enjoy it. Although I was all dressed and ready to leave, all I really wanted to do was put my pyjamas on and go to bed. I had to literally force myself to go out. It really is hard walking into a bar on your own, especially being female and unable to speak the local language. I fired up the Beast and gave myself a pep talk on the drive there, convincing myself this was all perfectly OK. I parked in an appropriate getaway spot and as I opened the van door, I dropped my mobile phone, it slid right under the belly of the Beast. Having found a kitchen utensil and crawled under the Beast to retrieve my phone I was now confidently strutting down the street towards the bar. As I got closer, I could see the bar, but as the windows were frosted, I couldn't see inside. I bit the bullet, pushed open the door and made my grand entrance. It was like a scene from the movie American Werewolf in London, it all went rather quiet as everyone turned to look at me. I imagined, as they were all staring at me, that they were thinking 'she's not local' 'she's a stranger in town'. But no, it wasn't that. Reality hit as I caught a glance of myself in the mirror behind the bar. My face was streaked with black oil and my white jumper had an interestingly placed black handprint upon it. There must have been an oil spill on the road when I'd crawled under the Beast. Trying to redeem myself I spotted Climon and shouted out "Bonsoir, Lemon": a word association I'd used to remember his name.

I didn't stay long. I hid myself at a table in the corner, nursing a small beer for as long as possible, and then discreetly left when the band started.

We got to go touring in the Beast for a few days this week. It was OK. If nothing else it gave me the undivided attention of Mee. When we're in the house Bear is constantly trying to get up close to Mee. He's always pushing in for her attention and I must admit it makes me a bit jealous when she strokes him. I've tried climbing up and sitting on her knee, but she seems to get a bit annoyed when I do this. Last night Mee was taking a bath and Bear even tried to squeeze through a hole in the door to join her. I thought: if you can't beat him, join him. But we both got our heads stuck and had to lie there until she got out the bath. I even thought that Bear was in our room last night, but luckily, it's just a big rat, living in the eaves.

Chapter 26

I woke to another frosty morning but thankfully the house was warm and cosy. Mr J had the heating running constantly at the moment and I was glad of this, although I think this warmth is what encouraged the creature living in the eaves to be so active. Even though I couldn't see him and I didn't know what he was, I'd got quite used to him coming out to play each night and had come to worry if I didn't hear him.

I'd taken Milo and Bear for their morning walk in the field and was walking back to the house to make coffee, but Bear was stalling. He'd found something of interest in the bushes so I wandered over to investigate. As I got nearer, I could see he'd found an old tatty football, but, when the football squealed, I realised it was in fact a hedgehog. I never knew hedgehogs could make so much noise. I managed to grab hold of Bear and drag him back to the house, much to his dismay. Back at the house while standing at the door waiting for Milo to catch-up, I heard a strange dripping noise at my feet, when I looked down, I could see Bear had cocked his leg and was actually peeing on my fake Ugg boot, no doubt my punishment for spoiling his game of football.

With a few more days to myself I was now preparing the Beast for another little jaunt. The Beast didn't need too much preparation when we went on our mini-adventures, just a top up of fresh water in the tank and a 'cabin secure for take-off' prep. Today we were going to La Ferte Mace, a destination I had Googled and decided would be fairly easy to find. I stopped off on the way at a supermarket to buy some provisions, but as usual had timed it wrong. For some strange reason all the shops in France close for a two-hour lunch. Could you imagine if Tesco did this? After sitting in the car-park for a long while we were now stocked up and ready to go again.

The drive to La Ferte Mace was pleasant enough and only took about an hour. We pulled into the town centre and parked up the Beast. I put Milo's lead on him and wandered into the town to explore, but it appeared the town had closed. There were plenty of shops but few of them were open and this wasn't anything to do with lunch breaks. I'd begun to realise that France was really struggling with this economic climate and businesses were suffering, the majority of them shut down for the winter months. There were hardly any people wandering about, pavement cafés held no activity other than a random pigeon and shops that were actually open had no customers, La Ferte Mace was like a ghost town. Having walked the town, twice, and seen nothing of interest we returned to the Beast. My sat-nav map showed me a lake nearby so we left the town and drove towards it. Unfortunately, the car-park at the lake had those dreaded overhead barriers in place so I had to make a ten-point turn manoeuvre and retreat. This in turn made me lose my bearings and I was now heading down a small dirt track with no idea where I would end up. But, as I'd often discovered on my travels, getting lost can be the best thing to happen. The end of the dirt track brought us into a small, secluded parking area right beside the lake with a sign welcoming overnight stays for motor-homes, result.

Milo bounced out the van, quite excited with our overnight location, as was I. The Beast neatly tucked up in a perfect spot, affording us a picture postcard view of the lake from our conservatory window. After walking the entire circumference of the lake, with a few dips in for Milo, we were now back in the van. With the sun setting across the lake in the distance and the light fading, I drew down all our blinds. I'd just cosied up with Milo on the couch when I heard a car outside, and then another car. I got up and peeped through a gap in the blinds. I could see two cars parked beside us and counted five teenage boys sitting on the bonnets. They were all smoking and their car stereos were competing with each other blasting out some familiar tunes. It's funny, because ordinarily I would have been quite unnerved by this display, but because they were all speaking French it all sounded so lovely. As I couldn't understand a word they were saying I chose to imagine they were all chatting about which library books they had borrowed this week and how much work they had all done on their school project. After about an hour they all piled back into their cars, did a few doughnuts around the car park, sprayed the Beast with gravel, and then headed home, no doubt to finish their school projects.

After two glorious nights beside the lake we returned to the house for a week of Le garçon duties and then before we knew it, we were back in the Beast for another couple of days exploring the joys of Normandy. This time we drove to La Suze-sur-Sarthe and stopped for three nights right on the edge of the River Sarthe. Another very pretty village, but yet again the village appeared to be closed. It seemed to be that the only business open was the bakers, and the only people walking through the village were the ones with baguettes under their arms. Our location was very peaceful camping beside the river, the only sound being an occasional boat passing by, oh, and, the church bells, my word they do like their church bells in France.

Our pattern continued; a week or so for Le garçon duties, then a few days travelling in the Beast. Northern France in the winter is rather beautiful, miles and miles of open countryside, quaint little villages with roads so tiny the Beast sometimes only just fitted through, and motorways with hardly any traffic upon them. I now felt completely confident driving through France in the Beast, and had begun to venture further afield.

Next destination – Saint Ceneri le Gerei, possibly the prettiest village we had discovered so far. It appeared time had stood still in this charming and picturesque setting. Home for two nights was a motor-home friendly spot just on a bend beside the now familiar River Sarthe. Once parked up my back-door opened right onto the meadow leading down to the river. Over to my left I could see a tiny medieval chapel which certainly deserved further inspection. With wellies on I traipsed up the field and entered the chapel. The inside was as enchanting as the outside, and I found myself imagining my dream wedding; me arriving at the chapel from a boat on the river, walking bare foot through the meadow, my soft silk wedding dress floating against the long grass, and looking up toward the tiny stone chapel, backdropped with rolling fields and towering trees, where I see my beau, stood tall in the doorway, waiting on me and besieged by my beauty. I was rudely awakened from my enchanted dream by Milo, barking furiously at the door, wanting in. Having signed the little guest book we headed off, up the hill, towards the village.

The village presented itself as a small cluster of charming houses and one open restaurant overlooking the river. Neatly cobbled streets led back down towards the river. Back at the van I sat on my back step, reading my book, and basked in the winter sunshine. A gentleman dog walker passed by and said hello, in English. A conversation ensued and it transpired the gentleman was an artist, living in the village, with his own studio. He then uttered one of the oldest and most cliched lines to date "Would you like to come up and see my etchings?".

"Yes, please." I replied.

I followed him up the hill, through the village, to his studio. Here, he took great pleasure in showing me all of his paintings on display and told me the background to each one. He was certainly an interesting character so when he suggested a drink, at the local restaurant later, I accepted.

Back in the van whilst freshening up in preparation for my 'date', I wondered to myself if this could be the start of a beautiful friendship?

Could he be the man at the chapel door? Milo was lying on the couch, watching me intently as I applied my lipstick, obviously in a mood with me; knowing he was not invited on this rendezvous.

I arrived before my gentleman friend and sat waiting at a table outside on the veranda. And then I saw him, walking down the road, hand in hand with his wife. My slightly broken heart soon mended with some much-missed female conversation: his wife was adorable. The three of us sat for hours, drinking local wine and exchanging interesting stories. All in all, a very pleasant afternoon.

Mee really needs to stop daydreaming. Every now and then she goes off into this make-believe world of loveliness and happy ever afters. I mean it's all well and good having a dream, I certainly do, mine usually involves a never-ending bowl of food. But life's not like that and she crushes herself every time she realises this. I do want her to be happy, I just wish there was more I could do to help her achieve that happiness.

Chapter 27

Life had fallen into a stress-free routine for Milo, Me and the Beast, here in France; wake early, make coffee, take Le garçon to bus stop, walk dogs, sit in Beast to write book, tidy house, prepare dinner, then watch Netflix movies all night. My few expeditions away from the house were not very exciting though. Don't get me wrong, ordinarily I loved being out and about in the Beast with Milo, but here everywhere was just a little bit too quiet. I wasn't meeting any eligible bachelors, and my now 3% fluency in French wasn't opening any doors for me. My rural location was certainly picturesque but had a lack of activity; grocery shopping at Intermarche was always uneventful, people-watching in pavement cafés was fruitless due to the lack of people and driving around in the Beast proved costly on the fuel tank. I was beginning to feel a bit bored and stagnated.

Mr J had gone away for a two-week period this time and having read every book I possessed and watched practically every movie on Netflix, I now spent hours hooked on other people's lives through social media. I had amassed hundreds of *friends* on Facebook, mainly through writing my blog, yet I didn't know any of them. But now feeling so bored, I was following all of their feed stories, on a daily basis, to fulfil my own life. It was gossip to me, and gossip seemed to be something I missed now. What was happening at their work, with their kids and in their relationships? I had no such conversation like this of my own, so I was prying into other peoples. It provided me with a small window of entertainment.

One particular story of interest came from a gentleman living near my home town in England. He'd written of a forthcoming road trip he had just booked with some of his friends. This road trip was called

Rust2Rome and involved purchasing a five-hundred-pound car and travelling from Edinburgh to Rome, via the Swiss Alps, in a convoy with about fifty other cars. I thought this sounded wonderful and wrote a comment on his page telling him so. He immediately wrote back: Come with us!

A private conversation ensued, on social media, with him trying to persuade me to join him and his friends on this amazing road trip. I took his conversation with a pinch of salt, but intrigued by the concept of this adventure I took a peek at the Rust2Rome website.

It stated; 'Rust2Rome is an adventure of a lifetime. It's you and your car taking to the road on a four and a half thousand-mile journey through Europe. You're doing it in a car that cost less than £500, in foreign countries on challenging roads. Rust2Rome will push you to the limits from start to finish. Remember the roads from movies like the Italian Job, Casino Royale and Ronin, those twisty one's going around the side of a mountain? That's the roads you'll be driving on. This isn't for the faint hearted. If you can handle it, you'll be rewarded by the sight of the Roman Coliseum at sunset after ten days of the most breath-taking driving you'll ever do. That is, if you make it. Each day the carefully planned route will take you to glorious high point whether an amazing monument, a city centre tour or a breath-taking road. You won't have heard of these places before, you won't find them in tour guides or holiday brochures, in fact you'll be lucky if they're mentioned on a map. It's a Top Gear adventure without the fifteen support vehicles. Your teams will meet up each day at a pre-booked camp-site, having enjoyed the peak of the day, to relax and tell everyone about it.'

When I'd finished reading, I felt this adventure had my name written all over it. An actual road trip, across Europe with like-minded people. Maybe this would be how I could meet my future husband? Or even just encounter a little romance? If nothing else it sounded like taking part could be so much fun.

Unfortunately, the cost involved was way above my budget so I pushed all thoughts of this road trip far from my mind. But my Facebook *friend* didn't. He was now messaging me daily trying his utmost to convince me that I must join his team. His team consisted of three men; himself, his best friend and his father. He insisted a female with a personality like mine was a must for the fourth seat in his car. He assured me it would cost me nothing as he would sponsor my place. He also happened to mention that his team would not be camping with the rest of the teams but had in fact booked hotel accommodation en-route. This being down to the fact that his father was in his eighties and would struggle with sleeping in a tent. Two twin rooms had been booked for each night, which meant: a spare bed was readily available for me.

"But you don't even know me, we are complete strangers," I pointed out.

"Nicci, I've read your blog, you are the perfect travel companion!" He argued.

Then I remembered, as my father had so often said to me 'a stranger is a friend you haven't met yet'. And so, crazy as it might be, I agreed to go with these three unknown men, in a £500 car, driving four and a half thousand miles through Europe on the trip of a life-time.

My *friend* was now contacting me on a regular basis with updates of the planned trip. He even offered to pay for my journey back to the UK and said he could provide a doggy sitter for Milo. I politely refused, bearing in mind I hadn't even told my family of this crazy idea. Of course, when I did eventually tell my family, they all said out loud what I had been thinking. "What's in it for him?"

I needed to ask him this question in a tactful manner. Having read my blog he would likely know that I was looking for love, but having got to know him a little over the last few days I felt quite certain it wasn't to be with him. But, and without being presumptuous, I didn't want him to think it could be. I needed to know that he wouldn't be expecting any 'hanky panky' on the road trip. Thankfully, he took my question in a gentlemanly fashion. He categorically assured me there would be no 'hanky panky' on his part and that he would be my perfect GBF. I wasn't quite sure what GBF stood for and wondered if it meant gay best friend?

So, with my decision made, my next adventure lay ahead. The hard bit would be telling Milo as sadly he would not be included in this adventure.

Here she goes again... 'We're going on an adventure Milo. Mee and you'... When will it all end, I wonder? This girl cannot sit still. Whoever said it's a dog's life never lived mine! I just begin to settle down and then she's off again. This time we're going back to England so that's not so bad. But then she threw in one of those curve balls: when we get back, she is going somewhere without me. Somewhere without me? That doesn't sound quite right.

I would never tell Mee, but to be honest, I'm secretly looking forward to the rest. I just want familiar surroundings and familiar faces. And I know I sound spoilt but I don't want to share my life with other dogs any more. Although, I will miss Bear, a little bit, I do enjoy it when he licks my ears. What I won't miss is him peeing on everything, me included, that dog has serious territory issues, I don't know if Mee knows, but Bear also pees on the wheels of our Beast every single morning...

Chapter 28

Spring made its first appearance here in France, snowdrops and daffodils popping up everywhere. Playing in the garden everyday with Milo and Bear now became a pleasant activity and I even felt excited to be doing the laundry; clean washing blowing on the line equals one of my guilty pleasures.

I'd spoken to Mr J of my planned road trip and he agreed it was a must. He would be sorry to see me go but could quite understand why. He could identify with my struggle of living in such a rural location and empathised with my loneliness. All he asked was that I could give him a few weeks to arrange alternative care for Le garçon. No problem, I told him.

I managed to fit in one more trip in the Beast before my departure from France. I'd found a perfect camping spot only about two miles away. It provided six large, free parking bays, free electricity and an unlimited supply of water. It also positioned us on the side of a lush green hill just above a beautiful fresh water lake. This was a tranquil location and Milo spent hours running up and down the hill retrieving his ball and then diving into the lake to cool off. Although the family of ducks did seem a bit peeved by this disturbance.

We spent two nights here and on the second evening I'd just settled down on the couch to read my new book, when I heard a rattling noise coming from the roof of my van. It was quite annoying and I couldn't ignore it. I knew it would probably be just a leaf blowing across the roof, but in this peace and quiet it sounded like a glass marble rolling on tin. The only access I had to inspect my roof was through the sky light in my kitchen. So, standing on my small, plastic, three-legged stool, with a kitchen spatula in hand, I poked my head out of the sky light. I could see the culprit straight away, a sycamore leaf impersonating a small helicopter. It was just slightly out of reach so I stretched my arm out with the spatula to try and flick it onto the ground. It was at this point I heard the sound of the plastic stool cracking under my weight and then suddenly it snapped under my feet, leaving me dangling in mid-air with just my head and one arm poking out the roof of the van. Milo, thinking we were playing some kind of game, was now barking at my heels and grabbing my trouser leg between his teeth. To make matters worse during this commotion, a couple out walking had stopped and were now staring up at my head poking out of the sky light. I smiled at them, waved my spatula in the air and shouted out a friendly 'bonjour!' just before I fell crashing to the floor, landing on top of Milo.

Back at the house Mr J and Le garçon had gone into town and I was sorting out my bedroom, ready for our return to the UK. I could hear the little creature in the eaves, scurrying around, and thought I'm really going to miss him when I leave. Milo and Bear were rolling around on the floor at my feet and Milo seemed to be enjoying having his ears licked by Bear, I wondered if Milo may miss Bear. Coming to France had been the right decision at the time, a decision I had made and followed through. And although France had been good to us over the last few months, it was not where I wanted to be. Had I been living in this beautiful, rural location with the man of my dreams I'm sure I could have lived out my life quite happily. But I was lonely and I was sad. It was time to move on.

With the Beast all packed up and ready to take us to Dieppe for our ferry crossing to Newhaven, I started the engine. We said our goodbyes to Mr J, Le garçon and Bear, with Mr J insisting we should return whenever we wanted.

And off we went. We had a trouble-free drive to Dieppe, without getting lost, it only took us a few hours. Boarding the Beast onto the ferry proved no problem either, although leaving Milo, below deck, once again, pulled at my heart strings.

On disembarking the ferry in Newhaven, I reset my sat-nav from kilometres to miles and then pressed the 'home' button. In my mind this was a fake button, I didn't have a home, well certainly not one of my own. But we always seemed to be welcome in someone's home, so home was where we were going.

Disembarking the ferry, it was nearing 10pm and the roads were dark and unfamiliar, also I initially confused myself with what side of the road I should be driving on and had a few near head-on collisions. My plan had been to stop in a safe place overnight and continue our journey in the morning, but in the dark I struggled to source a safe place. So, I kept driving and driving and driving. The roads were now so quiet of traffic, that before I knew it, I had driven for over three hours. But, now feeling tired and a bit concerned that the Beast might need a rest, I pulled into a service station just off the motorway.

The service station displayed signs everywhere stating hefty fines would be enforced if you parked for over three hours. So, having set my alarm clock for just under a three-hour period, I curled up on the couch with Milo and slept. At about 4am I was woken by the loud shrill of my alarm clock, and the noise of a juggernaut lorry roaring its engine beside me, not my usual calming silence of waking up in France.

It remained dark as we continued our journey up the motorway and Milo sat behind me the whole way in an unsettled manner, no doubt confused, travelling at this ungodly hour. But after a few more hours of driving and daylight dawning Milo began to recognise familiar sights. Being so early in the morning and knowing my family would still be sleeping, I drove the Beast straight to our local woods, a firm favourite of Milo's. Milo now bounced from couch to couch and began yelping at the window, he was so excited to be home. And I think I was too.

Having said my goodbyes to Mr J, Le garçon, Bear and the big rat in the eaves, I was now back in my favourite seat, behind Mee, in the Beast: we were heading home. I feel the same as Mee on the home front, I have no idea where it is, but as long as I'm with her and there is a food supply, I'm happy.

The drive back took forever, I thought she would never stop driving. Then I began to recognise a few familiar places and before I knew it, we were at 'my' woods. Oh, the joys! Royden Park is my territory, I grew up here, I remember the first day Mee brought me here; she was terrified to let me off my lead, thinking I might run off and leave her. As if.

We spent what felt like hours having a good wander around, and I even saw a few familiar faces; the little white scotty fella, the burly bulldog guy, and that extremely pretty one called Willow. I filled them all in on my adventures in France and even tried that 'bonjour' word on Willow: I think she was rather impressed. Maybe 3% impressed anyway.

Milo and Me chilling in The Beast

Milo and Me travelling through France in The Beast

Chapter 29

It was lovely to be back on the Wirral staying with Pip and her partner, and Milo settled in straight away. I spent the next few days enjoying sitting in cafés with Pip, doing our favourite past-time of people watching, with the added bonus of plenty of people to actually watch. I was also enjoying shopping in supermarkets and recognising all the products on the shelves. I also made time to catch up with all my family and friends, although I'm sure they were slightly irritated with my constant "Well, when I was in Frrraaaance...".

The Beast was safely parked up and enjoying a well-earned rest and I was missing him already. Driving about in the Beast on the open road always gave me a feeling of complete freedom and abandonment, and I already had itchy feet to take off again. But my Beast would have to wait, because I had my Rust2Rome trip to conquer yet.

I'd been back for a few days and had made arrangements to finally meet the three amigos whom I'd be travelling with on my road trip. Thankfully we all seemed to hit it off. JC, who'd invited me on the trip, was of an age with me, had a boyish personality and a love of cars. His life-long best friend, GT, was slightly older and possessed a wisdom of well-travelled knowledge. TC, was in his eighties and had a lifetime of experience as a motor mechanic. What quality I had to offer on this trip was a mystery to me; I wasn't a great driver; my sense of direction was useless and I didn't know a spark plug from a bath plug. But they all seemed keen for me to join them on this epic adventure, how could I say no?

The car we were all going to travel in was a Range Rover. I did not know they only cost £500... Our team name was 'Range Pig', reason being JC cooked hog roasts as a side-line. The Range Pig, car number 21, stood proud on JC's driveway all stickered up with local companies sponsoring our trip and our chosen charity: The Northern Lights Children's Charity. There was also a large pink sticker on the car bonnet advertising SheWee (a lady's portable toilet, no less) because during my own research for the trip, I had read that toilet stops were few and far between, so, I had written to SheWee and they had very kindly provided me with a bright pink one to take with me. Having read the leaflet, and as instructed practiced my SheWee in the shower, I did wonder if I would actually ever use it.

The banter written on the Facebook page for the Rust2Rome trip was now in full swing, the organiser, Marko, encouraging us all to get to know one another in preparation for our adventure. There appeared to be about 48 teams involved, amounting to nearly one hundred people mainly consisting of men. Result - I might yet find my husband. I had also roped in my three amigos to act as my wing men on the trip and they were all well aware of my 'husband material' list. I was now feeling quite hopeful about meeting someone on this adventure.

Trying to create a capsule wardrobe for the trip proved to be a difficult task, space in the Range Pig was limited, so we permitted ourselves one small luggage piece each. As we were travelling through Scotland, England, France, Switzerland and Italy I found it near impossible to pack for all climates. On one hand I wanted to look good, on the other I wanted to be warm and comfortable. I also decided it was very important to pack my LBD. If I was fortunate enough to meet the man of my dreams on this adventure, I wanted to be prepared: every girl should own a little black dress. Another item of clothing I wanted to get just right was my pyjamas: sharing a room with JC, I didn't want to give out the wrong message. So, buttoned up to the neck and reaching down to my ankles was my chosen attire. Having now been in the company of JC on a few occasions, I still had a niggling feeling he was maybe looking for more than just a travel companion. But I decided he was a good man and gentlemanly enough for me to handle.

I had a few mixed feelings about my forthcoming road trip. There was such a buzz of excitement surrounding it; the places we would visit, the roads we would travel, the people we would meet and of course the memories we would create. But travelling with three practical strangers, and without Milo filled me with some trepidation. Somehow, I managed to push my many 'what ifs' to the back of my mind and also recognise the fact that Milo would be perfectly fine staying with my family. I reminded myself that life is an adventure and opportunities present themselves in mysterious ways. Once again, I had an opportunity to do something different with my life, I would be foolish not to embrace it.

She's packed that suitcase about a hundred times and she still can't close the lid. And I'm getting a bit fed up with all the fashion shows. 'Yes, you look nice, No, your bum doesn't look big'. I try to pay attention, but to be honest I'm not that interested in what Mee looks like on this trip because I'm not going with her. She keeps giving me this guilty look and apologising for not taking me with her, but I really don't mind. I'm going to be staying with Pip and the Welsh Man and I'm jolly well looking forward to it. Pip is so easy to manipulate on the food front, I don't have to give her my sad eyes for very long before she succumbs and pops me a treat. And, although the Welsh Man winds me up a bit, especially when he tucks my ears into my collar, he is good fun to be around. I will miss Mee, she always knows how to reach that special spot with a knuckle rub in my ears, but she has nothing to feel guilty about, I'm going to be just fine.

Chapter 30

D-day was upon us. I'd spent the entire morning spending my time with Milo and storing up an abundance of hugs in preparation for our time apart. He didn't seem bothered at all, lying on the couch, hardly opening his eyes, as I tearfully walked out the door, suitcase in hand.

I was quite amazed we all fitted into the car, considering all the luggage four people required over a three-week period, plus all the maintenance tools. I took up my position, in the back, behind the passenger seat. JC was the driver, GT was up front as co-pilot and TC was in the back with me. And off we went. The first leg of our journey began with the drive from the Wirral, to the departure point in Scotland, about a five-hour drive in total. All cars were to meet under the Forth Road Bridge in Queensferry tomorrow morning, where we would be given our instructions for day one of our adventure.

My first warning sign of things to come occurred about twenty minutes into our journey: we broke down. The engine had seemingly overheated and we were now sitting on the hard shoulder of the M56 with the bonnet up. Having waited for the engine to cool down we continued our journey north towards Scotland. About two hours later we overheated again and spent a long hour in a service station, with the bonnet up, cooling down again. Eventually, we arrived at our pre-booked hotel in Queensferry, limped into the car-park and once again lifted the bonnet.

My three amigos were all standing at the bonnet, scratching their heads and discussing the mechanics of the engine. I took this opportunity to wander around the car-park, having spotted a few of the other team cars which would be with us on this rally. They were easily identifiable due to all the different stickers upon them. There was already a 'sticker bomb' game occurring, so grabbing a few of our pre-made Range Pig stickers, I joined in. During this exercise I found my favourite car: the one with a Tassimo coffee machine fitted into the footwell. I made a point of introducing myself to the four young men occupying this vehicle.

After much tinkering under the bonnet, we had some food and drink at the hotel bar and got to know a few of our fellow travellers. So far there seemed to be a really, good fun, mixed bunch of people going on this trip. I could see straight away we were all going to have a great adventure. There were even some other girls in the teams, so I was also looking forward to some girly conversation en-route. I buzzed with pride when a fellow traveller told me, he'd heard of my blog. When he added he'd heard me mentioned whilst listening to Scott Mills of BBC Radio 1, I buzzed a whole lot more. Possibly my finest accolade?

It was getting late and with an early start tomorrow planned for the morning we bid everyone goodnight and headed up to our rooms. As JC and I entered our room I immediately became aware that there was only one bed.

"This is not a twin room, JC." I stated, quite panicked.

"Hey, it's fine, Nicci, it's a big bed." He replied quite nonchalantly.

I locked myself in the bathroom and proceeded to quickly get dressed into my extremely unsexy pyjamas. I stood in the bathroom, looking in the mirror and told myself; this was fine, people share beds, nothing untoward will happen, you are in control, Nicci.

When I came out the bathroom JC had taken up his position on the right-hand side of the bed.

"Nice pyjamas, Nicci." He said grinning.

I placed my phone under the pillow, put another pillow between myself and JC and slipped myself under the duvet. I spent the night in a fitful sleep, practically hanging off my edge of the bed, listening to the constant snores from JC.

The next morning, I got up early and quietly dressed in the locked bathroom. All teams were departing in fancy dress attire. As a cost cutting exercise, I had adapted one of my everyday outfits of checked shirt, denim shorts, boots and a straw hat: and with my hair in bunches I was now Daisy Duke. TC was Spider Man and for some strange reason JC and GT were both wearing smart dinner jackets, extremely short shorts and ladies high heeled shoes. We made for a very odd foursome and attracted some strange looks at the breakfast buffet.

The starting point under the Forth Road Bridge was extra special for me because my best friend Sue had come to see me off. She only lived down the road in Perth, so had driven up to wave me off. There were hordes of people gathered under the bridge and so many different makes and models of cars parked up, even a hearse - fortunately with no dead people in it. With everyone milling around in their fancy-dress costumes introducing themselves, the atmosphere was electric. All the cars, decorated in their various stickers, were roaring their engines and honking their horns, eager to begin the adventure ahead.

Marko, the organiser, had given his welcome speech and handed out our Day 1 route sheets. These route sheets were to be handed out each morning at the camp-site, showing the GPS co-ordinates of our daily destinations and regular checkpoints for meeting places. Each checkpoint would be a place of interest and a chance for all 48 cars to re-connect. Because we were not staying on the camp-sites with the rest of the rally, GT had been allowed prior access to the planned route and had booked hotels as close as possible to each camp-site. I must admit I felt a little disappointed that we were not camping with the others, but I was nonetheless grateful to be on board.

Marko gave the starting signal and off we went, all 48 cars in convoy. I took up my back-seat position and enthusiastically hung out of the window videoing the snake of cars crawling up the hill. On reaching the main road the convoy of cars dispersed and it was time to tune into the CB radio channel we had all been given. The banter on the radio waves immediately reflected the camaraderie of our journey ahead: this was going to be an epic adventure.

Exactly one hour into the journey our car was in a familiar spot: the hard shoulder of the motorway. Parked beside the fast-flowing traffic with Spider Man tinkering under the bonnet, flanked either side by two big men, half dressed as women, I, Daisy Duke, chose to stay inside the vehicle watching the passing cars slow down to peer at this strange sight.

Back on the road we somehow managed to re-join the convoy in the Lake District and the Range Pig came into its own on the steep and winding roads through the mountains. Other cars were struggling on the sharp bends and steep inclines, especially the hearse. But having a four-wheel drive Range Rover, we were now the lead car. Having taken the lead, we were also the first car to arrive at the camp-site. I sat waiting in the Range Pig excited to see the other cars begin to arrive and start to set up their camp-site, I envisaged an evening of camp-fire frivolity ahead. But my team decided it had been a long day and we should now head to our pre-booked bed and breakfast, ready for day two.

The sweet little old lady at the bed and breakfast establishment showed us to our room. And yet again I saw only one bed. As JC enthused at the two chocolate mints placed on the drinks tray: I began to feel like I was on some kind of weird honeymoon.

Day two began with a good old-fashioned cooked breakfast, then we all piled back into the Range Pig to continue our journey towards the Port of Dover. Due to the temperamental condition of our engine, my team chose to forgo the GPS co-ordinates and take a direct route on the motorway. With the rain falling heavily and the dreariness of the drive I began to fall asleep. But I was suddenly jolted awake by the sound of JC swearing loudly. I could see our windscreen wipers had completely failed and I held my breath as JC blindly swerved across three lanes of high speed, motorway traffic, to reach the safety of the hard shoulder. I take my hat off to JC: his swift and experienced driving skills saved us from untold disaster in that moment. Luckily, on the hard shoulder, we could see an exit slip road just ahead and crawled along it to reach the nearest service station. Under the cover of the garage forecourt, Spider Man managed to fix the broken wipers and our journey continued.

Arriving at the next camp-site in Dover we sat in our car watching the other teams set up camp, in the pouring rain, and I questioned my desire to be camping with them. We didn't stay long and headed to our next, one bedded, hotel room. I cheered myself up with a Skype call home. Pip made me laugh when she told me about Milo; apparently, he did not know Pip had two cats living in her house. They tend to spend most of their days hiding in Pip's bedroom, which Milo is not allowed into, and only venture out at night. But every now and then Milo spots them, barks like mad and runs to Pip, to tell her of these cats; each time he acts as if this is new information and that she might not know there are intruding cats in her house. Pip's partner says Milo is behaving like a goldfish: with a three second memory.

Day three and another early start with a ferry crossing to Calais. This gave me a perfect opportunity to mingle with the other teams for a few hours on the ship, and the bonus of finding a free tasting Vodka bar. I got friendly with some of the other team members and whilst we all sat, drinking our free vodka, they added me into their chat group on Facebook Messenger. Little did I know that I would not see them again until the end of the rally.

I felt a bit sad when Mee left to go on her road trip, but I couldn't let her know, otherwise she would have never left. I know she was having second thoughts about going, so I couldn't add to her woes by behaving like her and crying like a baby. She gave me so many hugs before she went and still insisted on giving me that stupid story about going to the shops, makes me laugh does that. I hope her adventure is all that she hopes for and I really hope she finds that man she thinks she needs.

I'm having a great time here, although my walks with Pip are a bit shorter than the ones Mee takes me on. Arthritis they call it, but fair dos to her for making the effort. Every night, Pip makes a massive picnic for the Welsh Man to take to his work and every night when he returns from his work, I get given his left-overs. I'm in heaven.

Chapter 31

We were now in France. Calais to be precise, a location I had been in only a few months previously. It didn't look much different and we were now all in a convoy leaving the ferry terminal, with our next set of GPS co-ordinates. I should have known better than to think we would be travelling in a convoy with this fun and crazy bunch of UK plated cars. We lost them and the CB radio contact within the hour, as we were now sitting in a service station, with the familiar site of the bonnet up.

This turned out to be my first opportunity to use my SheWee. In typical French fashion the public toilet was just a hole in the floor, not pleasant. My SheWee actually worked a treat, but unfortunately the automatic flush system caught me off guard: water splashed boots.

It appeared our mechanical problem was quite serious so we drove to a nearby hotel in Saint Quentin where we spent the next two nights and three days holed up. Over the next few days much tinkering occurred under the bonnet and many long conversations were had about head gaskets, coolant leaks, radiators and thermostats. Phone calls were made back and forth to the UK and every man and his dog had the best advice to give. Most of these conversations went right over my head and I was of no use nor ornament to the team. The hotel we were in stood in the middle of a boring trading estate but after two days, having read two books and drunk endless cups of the free coffee provided in reception, I decided to take a wander further afield, around the trading estate. And this is where I spotted our knight in shining armour. A gentleman wearing a jacket emblazoned with the BMW logo and with the distinct look of a motor mechanic. After overcoming the language barrier, and having a good look under our bonnet, he took us to a local garage where a large supply of k-seal was purchased to enable our journey to continue.

And continue it did. For a while. We managed to travel about 80 kilometres before, once again, we overheated and this time spent about four hours in a service station, waiting for the engine to cool. Once cooled down GT found us another, remotely placed, hotel not too far away, where we stayed for one night.

The next day we were all feeling a little bit more optimistic. JC had decided that if we didn't drive too fast the engine didn't overheat. Driving through France, at an average speed of 50 miles per hour, reminded me of my time driving in the Beast, and I did wish we were all in him now. We were now plodding along, getting quite used to the irate trail of cars stuck behind us, and at last seemed to be clocking up some mileage. All was going quite well, that is until, dramatically we experienced total brake failure. Once again JC's faultless driving skills brought us safely onto another hard shoulder and the bonnet was lifted. After JC and TC had done some work under the bonnet to fix the brakes, GT announced he had Googled a not too far away Land Rover garage. Surely our problems could be resolved there?

We eventually arrived at the Land Rover garage and all traipsed inside. After what seemed like forever, Land Rover garage team told us they couldn't help us: but they knew a man who could.

What happened next involved a French gentleman arriving in his own, old and battered Land Rover, who in his broken English said 'follow me'. We duly obeyed and proceeded to follow him, seemingly back the way we'd just travelled, through small country lanes, for roughly an hour and a half. We struggled to keep up with him at times, all the while aware we could overheat or encounter brake failure again at any point. Eventually we arrived at a rambling old farmhouse, down a long dirt track and could see before us various abandoned and broken Land Rovers scattered around his property. It looked like a Land Rover grave yard and I did wonder if this would be where our journey ended?

The man slid open a large barn door and directed the Range Pig inside and onto a ramp. Land Rover man and the Range Pig team agreed upon a price and two more men appeared to begin the work. I took a little wander while this work took place and came upon another barn. Sneaking inside I found what I could only describe as a car enthusiasts paradise. There were dozens of old cars, some in view and some under dust sheets, some were probably dating back to the 1920's and all were in various states of repair. I have a complete ignorance when it comes to classic cars, but even I was impressed with this collection.

With the work now completed on the Range Pig, involving a very important spare part which had been salvaged from a dead Land Rover and fitted into the Range Pig, apparently, we were declared fit to drive. I think we still had some overheating issues so we still had to drive slowly. The Range Pig slowly took us to Vesoul, a town not too far away, where I was delighted to discover our hotel room had two beds. I star shaped all night and slept like a baby.

I've just had a great weekend and I'm thoroughly exhausted. The Welsh Man's little girl came to stay with us and she is so much fun to be with. She's like a smaller, younger version of my Mee. She rolls about on the floor with me chucking my tennis ball in the air and when she hugs me, she wraps both her arms around my whole body, just like Mee does. The Welsh Man even let us go to the local park together, although he was stressing a bit, and I'm sure I saw him hiding in the bushes at one point. I hope it was him in the bushes, because, when I did my business on the grass the little girl pulled a face and ran away. Maybe he picked it up for her?

The weekend went far too quickly, I didn't want the little girl to leave. When she was saying goodbye, I lay down on the floor, with my head flat on my front paws, looking up at her with my big sad eyes. It worked. She came back in, possibly half a dozen times, for just one more hug. Gets them all, every time.

Chapter 32

The hotel in Vesoul had an excellent wifi connection and enabled me to catch up with all the goings on with the rest of the rally. I could see from the group chat on Facebook Messenger all that I had missed out on so far. My roadside stops, garage forecourts and motorway service stations counted for nothing compared to their tales of adventure on tight winding roads, high in the hills within the convoy of the rally, not to mention their exhilarating nights of fun filled banter at the camp-sites. Well, I told myself, all is not lost, I am on a road trip: of sorts.

The next leg of our journey saw us leave France and enter Switzerland. I had been so looking forward to this part of the journey as Switzerland was a destination I had never visited. We hadn't broken down on leaving France but, alas, we did on arriving in Switzerland, just as we crossed the border. JC had the nous to pull off the road, before we entered one of the many long tunnels that wind through the mountains of Switzerland. I stood, in possibly, the prettiest lay-by so far, watching my three amigos yet again tinkering under the bonnet. It didn't look good: we had overheated, again. After another long wait for the engine to cool down, I suggested JC should type into the sat-nav 'local garage'. And now we were driving up a steep Swiss mountain road, going goodness knows where. We stopped off for a photo opportunity beside a poppy field, I was so happy; the views were amazing and I felt like a proper 'Heidi', standing high on the side of a Swiss mountain.

Our 'local garage' turned out to be pretty amazing too. It was a Volkswagen dealership and I stood and watched the Range Pig lifted up on the hydraulic ramps, operated by a mechanic, who looked as if he had dressed for a surgical procedure; pure white overalls, clean white hygiene gloves and not a spot of oil to be seen upon him. Even the equipment reminded me of a hospital operating theatre, all shiny and new, looking as if it had never been used. The surgeon, I mean mechanic, then proceeded to meticulously hoover the engine and pour some lovely pink liquid into the pipes. Again, a cash price was agreed, and our journey continued.

Before I knew it, we had left Switzerland and were now in Italy. We hadn't even stopped. But at least I could now say I had been to Switzerland.

Italy. Possibly my favourite place in the whole world. I'd visited many places previously in Italy and loved and adored everything about it; the scenery, the food and of course the sexy Italian men. In my eyes they just had that something about them which oozed sex appeal; the way they looked, the way they dressed and the way they spoke. I sat relaxed, in my back seat of the car, staring out of the window, merrily daydreaming of meeting my Italian Stallion.

Spending the entire journey in the back of the car with TC was like being the kids on the family holiday. Although we were very well-behaved children and never once asked, 'are we there yet?'.

I don't quite know where we were meant to be at this point, in Italy. Our final destination had always been Rome, but as all hope was lost of ever re-joining the rally, we now seemed to just be driving aimlessly.

Our aimless driving took us to Como, a place I'd been to a few times before and one which held some precious memories for me. This is where I first learnt how to water-ski, on Lake Como and also spent an evening dancing Salsa with the locals in an outdoor arena. The scenery around the lakes takes your breath away and if I remember correctly, George Clooney lives in a mansion beside the lake. Yes, this pit-stop was going to be a good one, I thought to myself.

Our hotel for tonight was clean and modern but unfortunately miles away from civilisation. And, we were back to sharing a one bedded room. That night we all sat together in one room, had pizza delivered and watched a James Bond movie. Not quite the evening I had anticipated.

The next day, we left Como early and continued our drive South. We were still sticking to main motorway routes and still driving at about 50 miles per hour. Having read all the books I'd brought with me, I found myself sleeping a lot in the back seat, usually dreaming of what exciting stuff the other teams were no doubt getting up to.

We weren't making much headway, limping down the motorway, so GT suggested we stop overnight in Florence. Yes! I love Florence, having been here before and remembering it as being romantic and enchanting. Also, GT knew of a little place, on the hillside above Florence, named Fiesole. And what a gem this turned out to be. Perched high in the hills this delightful, bijou village full of pavement cafés bustling with tourists and scattered with market stalls. The spectacular views over the city of Florence were breath-taking and stepping out of the car, I welcomed the cooler air on my face.

We found our quaint hotel tucked up one of the many steep and tiny streets and, as per, JC handled the car with ease. That evening we all took a wander down to the square and after a mooch around the market stalls we took up residence in a pavement café. I was in my element, not just with my all-time favourite dish of spaghetti Carbonara, but with all the people. My appetite for people watching was more than satisfied here.

My dish of Carbonara tasted delicious, I savoured each and every mouthful and devoured the whole plate in no time. I complimented my dish with a bottle of fine Italian wine and finished off with a bowl of home-made ice cream. My food budget for this trip had been meagre, I had tried to account for every penny I spent and always tried to choose the cheapest dish on the menu. I'd had the foresight, to pack in my suitcase, a few packets of ginger biscuits, for any hungry spells, but they had been finished days ago. To be fair, GT had more often than not included me in their food and drink budget and I was grateful for his kindness. But tonight, I had no hesitation to blow most of what remained of my budget.

Our stay in Fiesole was far too short, but I promised myself this was a place I would certainly re-visit. We were now back on the road and on the final leg of our road trip.

Rome. Italy's hot-blooded capital; an inspiring cosmopolitan city steeped in romantic culture and history. I'd been fortunate enough to have visited Rome twice before and was so excited to be returning.

The Colosseum was the final destination checkpoint of the Rust2Rome car rally and, unwittingly, we were the first car to arrive. Having begun our epic journey 10 days ago, in Edinburgh, as part of a convoy of 48 cars, we were now a lone car at the finish line. It had never been a race, there were no winners, it was all about the taking part. But somehow, I felt like I had been part of nothing.

My three amigos had been absolute troopers, they had invested so much time and energy into this road trip and never once got grumpy. Even though I had felt like excess baggage throughout the whole journey, they had never taken the decision to offload me: although I'm sure they thought about it at times.

I'd begun this journey with the vision of it being 'the trip of a lifetime'. I had pictured myself as a driver; In France, having conquered the Paris traffic system, standing beneath the Eiffel Tower surrounded by my team mates; In Switzerland, driving at high speed, zigzagging treacherous mountain roads, in convoy, through the alpine scenery; In Italy, driving lazily through olive groves by day and living it up at night in vibrant

Italian bars. And every evening hanging out with my fellow travellers, camping under the stars, recalling all of the day's events.

What I'd got was; a long, tedious drive spent entirely in the back seat of an extremely temperamental car, with three men I barely knew or had got to know, taking in the views of endless motorway service stations and garage forecourts. My nights were spent sleeping on the edge of a bed listening to the snores of my distant companion. I felt as if I had travelled this journey alone and had often pined for the company of Milo and the Beast.

But. I'd. Done. It.

This.

Once again, I'd made a decision to do something and this I had done.

I don't know if Pip knows, but there were two cats in her bedroom today. I've seen them before and I did tell her, I think. Today, I was just casually walking past her room, minding my own business when I saw something out of the corner of my eye. I stopped and poked my head into her room and there they were, bold as brass, just sitting on her bed, looking right at me. Trouble is, Pip had gone out to the shops (she also does that daft shop/biscuit/hug thing, just like Mee) so I barked quite loudly at them for a bit, but they didn't leave. As I'm not allowed in Pip's room, I made a mental note to inform her of these intruders upon her return.

Chapter 33

Pulling into our camp-site, situated on the outskirts of the city centre, I could see its sign above the entrance; aptly named 'Fabulous'. At that moment that is how I felt: Fabulous. We had actually reached the end of the road trip. Tonight, we would sit together as a group of nearly one hundred people, and celebrate completing the journey we had each travelled. Tonight, my three amigos had chosen to remain on the camp-site, mainly because no tents were involved. This was a *fabulous* camp-site and everybody involved in the Rust2Rome trip had been booked into a purpose-built chalet. Marko, the organiser, stood at the gate on our arrival, camera in hand and photographing each team car as it drove into the camp-site. I could see the look of surprise on his face as his camera captured our arrival. Nobody thought we would reach the finish line. Everybody in turn told us how surprised they were to see us here.

Our little chalet was just that: little. But I was rewarded with the luxury of not only having my own bed, I also had my own bedroom. Mind you, the thinness of the walls meant I was likely going to spend the night listening to not one, but three amigos snoring.

Having freshened up I sat outside on our veranda, sipping a beer and waiting for the boys to get ready. I had intended to wear my little black dress for this evening's celebrations, having spent the last ten days mostly looking like a scruffy, old and haggard Daisy Duke, but unfortunately my LBD hadn't fared well, squashed into the bottom of my suitcase.

After the boys had spent, what felt like forever, fussing around, we were now walking down to the restaurant to meet our fellow rally members. Just as we entered the restaurant, I could see the whole group lined up and posing for the finale group photograph. We had even managed to miss that.

We all sat down to dinner and I chose to join a large group of rowdy young men seated near the bar. I sat, transfixed by each of their stories, all of them recalling what a truly amazing adventure they'd experienced. They each had a tale to tell, an anecdote from a favourite checkpoint, a private joke of a certain car, a shared experience of many a tremendous road. In fact, they all had so many wonderful memories of their road trip, that they were now discussing booking another one for next year.

I had no stories to share with them, I had nothing of interest to tell. I left them with their discussion of next year's trip and went to sit with my three amigos. My three amigos were also in deep discussion: about the drive back home. My heart sank. The thought of spending another week in the car, breaking down every two hours, filled me with dismay.

I found a quiet corner in the restaurant and Skyped Pip.

As soon as Skype connected I saw an image of Pip and her partner seated on their sofa with Milo curled up in-between them. I just burst into tears.

"I want to come home, Pip, I want to come home now." I cried into the screen.

Pip had always been like a sister taxi for me. It didn't matter what time of night it was, she would drop everything and just jump in her car to come and pick me up. Admittedly, I was usually drunk and incoherent, but she never refused my calls of distress. She would always say to me, before I went on a night out "Call me if you can't get a taxi." But this was different. I was over four thousand miles away, I couldn't just walk to the end of the street and wait for the welcome sight of her headlights driving towards me.

But, in typical Pip fashion, she spoke magic words.

"I'll book you a flight home, leave it with me and I'll e-mail you the booking tomorrow."

"I love you Pip." I squealed. "Hug Milo for me and tell him I'll be home soon."

The next day, I woke early and in a good mood. Pip had booked me a flight back to Liverpool for tomorrow and had told me to just pay her back when I could. So, in one more sleep I would be back with my Milo. I think my three amigos were also secretly relieved I would not be travelling back with them in the Range Pig.

Because the rest of the rally teams had spent the last ten days doing some pretty hardcore driving and sleeping in tents each night, they all chose to chill by the pool for the whole day. As we had in comparison spent the last ten days driving, at an average speed of 50 mph and sleeping in comfortable hotel rooms each night, we chose to take an open top bus tour of Rome's city centre.

As we hopped onto the bus, I noticed that strangely JC and GT were both wearing matching shiny pointed red shoes, thankfully not high-heeled. I chose not to make any funny comments as they had very kindly paid for my bus ticket. TC had chosen to remain in the chalet for a day of relaxation - or maybe he just didn't own a pair of shiny red shoes?

The open top bus tour came as a breath of fresh air for me. I got to take plenty of photos of all the historic Roman sights and drank in the beauty of it all. We stopped off at the Trevi Fountain and threw our obligatory coin into the water. I made my wish and it very nearly came true when a very sexy Italian policeman wrapped his arms around my waist as I took a selfie photograph. But before I had a chance to get to know him better, off he flew in hot pursuit of a pesky pick pocketer.

After a few hours of sight-seeing we stopped at a small bar in the corner of a bustling piazza. The bar staff were extremely friendly and happily plied us with copious amounts of alcohol. A political demonstration occurring outside had attracted crowds of people in the piazza and whilst everyone stood checking out the antics of the demonstrators, I was scanning the crowd looking for my sexy Italian policeman. Alas, he was nowhere to be seen.

Late into the evening, GT managed to get us exclusive entry to the roof top terrace of a luxury hotel he had stayed in many years ago. From here, we had an uninterrupted panoramic view across the whole of Rome at night. GT had pushed the boat out and ordered a bottle of the best champagne to celebrate this auspicious moment. I stood, sipping my champagne, looking across the romance of the city below me, the stars twinkling in the black sky above me, and JC behind me, retching into the champagne bucket.

Tonight, was a bit sad. I was curled up on the couch, in-between Pip and the Welsh Man, when suddenly I saw Mee's face. Skype, they call it. I felt like I'd been caught red handed, cheating on Mee. She looked all teary eyed and was blubbering on about wishing she was with us.

Pip was so good at calming her down and said all the right words. Mee was smiling when she said goodbye. It looks like Mee will be home very soon, which is wonderful news. I think Pip is finding it a struggle to walk with me every day, I do try and go extra slow, but she still finds the need to sit down on nearly every bench we pass.

Reading between the lines, I don't think Mee has had the adventure she was hoping for. She's done that thing again: Where fools rush in. She's been doing that a lot lately, I think I need to have words with her. This panic she's got about not having her 'happy ever after' is beginning to interfere with her here and now. I think Mee is a lovely human being and if she just stood still for a moment, I'm sure the whole world would see that too.

Chapter 34

Departure day. I'd got up really early and taken my shower before my three amigos woke. Now, having taken an early morning stroll around the camp-site, I took a seat in the sunshine, sipping Italian coffee outside the café at reception. I watched everybody busily prepping for the start of their journey, driving back to the UK. Cars were being tinkered with, provisions being bought from the camp-site supermarket, luggage being crammed into car-boots. Various people were milling around the reception area, swapping contact details, and making promises of re-union parties. I was overhearing conversations of; 'you're like family to me.' and 'we're going to be friends for life'. There were group hugs and tearful goodbyes, people's emotions were in overdrive and nobody wanted to leave.

I sat, on the edge, looking in on this display of camaraderie. I felt like an uninvited guest at a private party. I felt so envious of what they had all experienced over the last couple of weeks, of the adventure they would reminisce about for years to come. I finished my coffee and slowly walked back to our chalet.

Back at the chalet the three amigos were piling the last of their belongings into the Range Pig. My little suitcase sat on the edge of the veranda, looking as lonesome as I felt. I hugged each of my three amigos, in turn, and wished them a safe drive home. JC locked the chalet door and handed me the key, asking if I could drop it off at reception before I left.

"JC, can I ask you; why you invited me on this road trip?" I asked, curious to know.

"Nicci, it's just nice to be nice." He answered. And he was right. It was nice of him to invite me, it was nice to be included as part of their team and it was nice of them to put up with me. JC was a jolly nice man. All three of my amigos were.

I watched as they drove off in the Range Pig on their long drive home, I kept waving until they disappeared out of sight. And to this day, I've never seen them again.

With a few hours to kill before my bus ride to the airport I went and sat on a sun lounger beside the pool. I'd found some English books at reception and sat back, with a large chocolate ice cream in hand and did what I did best: relaxed in my own company. I really am quite a loner, I thought to myself. I'd spent my whole life wanting to be part of the party when in fact I was perfectly happy on my own. I think this is why I enjoyed travelling with Milo, in the Beast; I could dip in and out of other people's lives, and yet be happy in my own company, with Milo, always by my side. Was this why I struggled so much to find my perfect man? How can I share my life with someone when I am so happy on my own? What man would want me, knowing I was happy even when he wasn't there? I had some serious issues to work through if I was ever going to find myself a man who could put up with me. I'm a misfit, I decided.

The flight back to the UK was problem free, although I did half expect the pilot to pull over and lift the bonnet at times. Walking out of the terminal building at Liverpool airport I was greeted by Pip with open arms. I felt so happy to see her and couldn't wait to get back to her house and see Milo.

In the car on the drive back, Pip suggested I move in and live with her for a while. She'd spoken with the rest of the family and they all agreed that I needed to stay still for a bit. They all thought as I'd done so much travelling over the last couple of years it was now maybe time to stop, take a breath and think. Think? Did they not know that's what I did 24 hours a day? Hmm.

Back at Pip's and Milo's behaviour towards me really tested my emotions. He had chosen to give me the cold shoulder and I couldn't blame him. Every day he'd walk right past me acting like I was invisible and take up residence on the couch in between Pip and her partner. Here, he'd rest his head on Pip's lap and slyly watch me out the corner of his eye. If we were returning from the shop's I'd be the last person he'd greet on walking through the door. At bedtime he would, almost reluctantly, follow me with his head hung low. I had to put up with this behaviour for a few days, reminding myself he'd enjoyed weeks of relaxation with a calm and peaceful routine each day. He had been taken on his favourite familiar walks, he didn't have to share his home with other dogs, he didn't wake up each morning wondering where the Beast would take him next and every visitor to the house was a known person, who always gave him a treat. No wonder he didn't seem pleased to have me back in his life.

After a few days of me constantly pampering him, Milo let me back into his life. Relief was an understatement; Milo was my soul mate, my companion and my best friend. I didn't care where I was in the world as long as Milo was by my side. Dramatic, I know, but the bond I had built with this dog was difficult to understand: unless you were Mee.

My decision had been made. I would stay at Pip's for the foreseeable future and settle into some kind of normal lifestyle. But. Not without some sort of adventure included: I had applied to take part in a TV show. And, I had been accepted! The TV show called 'This Time Next Year' was presented by the lovely Davina McCall. The concept of the show was; people would appear on the show and make a pledge of what they personally wanted to achieve by this time next year. They would be

186

filmed, over the year, showing how they had achieved their goal. But the beginning, the middle and the end of the filming would all be *glued* together and shown as an elapsed time format on television.

My pledge was quite simple: I wanted to find my husband. Surely with a major television company involved and all of their resources to hand this pledge could be accomplished?

"Nicci, tell me, how do you intend to go about finding yourself a husband?" the TV researcher asked me during the selection process.

"Do you not provide one for me?" I ignorantly asked.

I have to admit I had never watched this television show before. I honestly thought *they* would have some 'husbands' available for me to choose from. I didn't think I would have to go out there and find one myself. But no. Here I was right back to where I had started, two years ago, and going on a journey looking for my husband. Only this time my whole journey was going to be filmed and broadcast on national television.

But I'd made a commitment and I would follow it through. I had decided to do This and This is what I would do. What did I have to lose? Nothing. So, here is to: This Time Next Year I *might* have a husband...

Mee's back. And she's all over me like a rash. I did miss her, I missed her dreadfully every single day. But I couldn't let her know that. Oh no. So, I did this reverse psychology trick and pretended I wasn't all that pleased to see her. I must admit it was hard; seeing her sad little face peering at me as I lay cuddled up next to Pip, ignoring her when she returned from the shops, and pretending to drag my feet to follow her to bed at night. Yes, that was hard. But it's paid off! We're staying where we are for the foreseeable future.

I've loved travelling around with Mee, in the Beast, and I have, mainly, enjoyed all the various homes we've been welcomed into. But I'm a bit tired now and I need a rest. And to be perfectly honest so does Mee. She needs a bit of normality back in her life.

Although in saying that, she sat me down this morning and said:

"Milo, we're going on an adventure, Mee and you. We're going to find me a husband, right here on our doorstep..."

Rust2Rome start line Forth Road Bridge

Rust2Rome finish line Colosseum Rome

THE END, for now

Nicci Taylor © 2019

What happens next ....

After The Beginning and The Middle, surely book three should be The End? The End would predictably read: and they all lived happily ever after. And me, I would certainly question ~ after what? And the answer would be: after this. They all lived happily ever after; this adventure, this journey, this collection of moments, this abundance of memories, this path of discovery.

And this is something I do not want to end.

So, what happened next is this: And they all lived happily doing this...

Please feel free to contact either myself or Milo at;

niccitaylor1@gmail.com

Thank you for reading my book. We would love to receive your feedback;

https://kdp.amazon.com/en_US

https://www.goodreads.com/

Good or bad I can take it, although Milo is slightly sensitive to criticism.

You can read our full blog and keep up with the latest antics of Milo and Me here;

http://miloandme6.blogspot.co.uk/

You can follow us on Twitter at;

https://twitter.com/nicci66nicci

See the Big Beach House;

https://www.facebook.com/casabrancaguesthouse

Shout-outs; book two

Just a few of the many organisations who helped create our adventure;

Gumtree – for the Beast and France

Wirral Small Cars – for the TLC you gave the Beast

RAC - for keeping the Beast on the road

P & O Ferries – for sailing the Irish Sea

Garmin satnav – for pointing us in the right direction

The Caravan and motor-home Club - for many a good night's sleep

Irish Tourism - for providing some stunning locations

Burns Pet Food - for keeping Milo well fed

Prostate Cancer - for helping my Daddy

RTE Ireland – for highlighting our adventure

Virgin Media Television (formerly TV3 Television) - for highlighting our adventure

Twofour Group – for continuing to highlight our adventure on ITV

Rust2Rome – for an unusual road trip

IanDavid Hair – for taming my locks

Facebook - for new friends and old

Twitter - for new friends and old

Nicci and Milo are currently residing on the Wirral. Milo has certainly slimmed down of late and Nicci has recently become a 'glamorous grandmother'. Sadly, The Beast had to be sold to help pay Nicci's bloomin credit card. Saying goodbye to The Beast broke Nicci's heart and she pines for him every day.

Life continues to treat Nicci and Milo well, and who knows what their next adventure will be...

Printed in Great Britain
by Amazon